Open Your Eyes to Joy

By
Jeffrey Cline

Printed in the United States of America

First Printing February 2019

ISBN 978-1-68454-852-1 Paperback

Published by: Book Services
www.BookServices.us

Contents

Dedication

To my wife, Nancy, for encouraging me in my writing and for being my patient and dedicated caregiver, bringing me through several near-death experiences, so that I am still here and able to compose this book.

To Dr. Roy Jones, my lead doctor at MD Anderson for five years, who, with the assistance of multitudes of other doctors, nurses, and administrative staff, directed me through numerous crises, so that I have a life.

To my late parents, Pat and Ruth Cline, who provided examples and wisdom through my life, resulting in the strong emotional foundation necessary to not just survive a crisis, but to strive for a better life afterward.

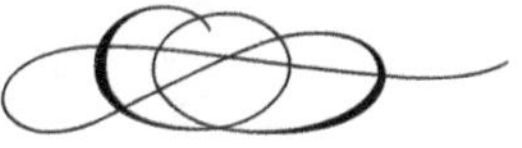

Contributors of Ideas, Stories, and Support

Fellow bicycling buddies and Christians James Deitiker and Tim and Kathy Coble, who provided important insight, wisdom and support.

Bob Vaught, Gary and Ann Murphy, Phil Baxter, Joy Alice Morrow—fellow Christians with seemingly preternatural wisdom, who helped to develop the definitions and methods.

Ted Robertson, Sean Kouplen, and Jim Stovall, who either wrote their own story, provided background information, or consented to be subjected to my interviews so that I could document the stories. They set forth the wisdom and essential elements to manage and grow happy, successful businesses.

Friend and author M.J. (Martha) Sherman, who inspired me to write the book and helped with the process.

Richard Study and Jack Camp: loyal, dedicated friends and caregivers who inspired me and helped me to survive the cancer.

Bob Warwick, Director of Crossroads Counseling and my good friends, who brought a Christian perspective to inspire me concerning those families and individuals in crisis.

The anonymous contributors who gave so much of their time, providing their stories, their wisdom, and their path of emerging from many different crises to have better lives.

Operation Hope Christian Prison Ministry provided their staff-time to set forth heartening, positive stories of past incarcerees recently released and rehabilitated.

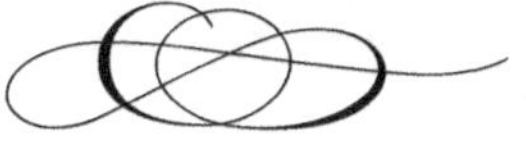

Preface

In his book *You Don't Have to Be Blind To See,* Jim Stovall, the blind, award-winning inspirational writer and speaker says, "Being blind isn't the worst thing that can happen to people. Living without hope is the worst thing." This book is about finding and using hope, faith, and positive attitude as tools to heal and find joy and happiness when you have been overcome by emotional and physical pain and despair. My credentials? A five-year fight for my life that included four near-death experiences. But I'm not just sharing my own experiences in this book. You will also find the stories of others who have found joy after severe setbacks of many kinds in their lives.

My heartfelt desire is that the stories, lessons, and practical techniques I share here will help you to follow the Reverend Martin Luther King Jr.'s advice and "carve a tunnel of hope through the dark mountain of disappointment."

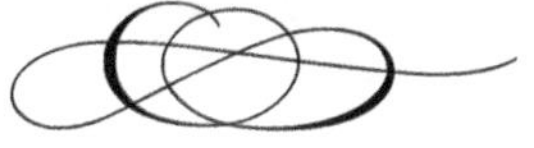

Chapter 1

Hanging by a Gossamer Thread

In heart-stopping shock, we heard the oncologist announce over the phone, "The test results are back. Get to the MD Anderson emergency room immediately. You are in the late stages of acute myeloid leukemia (AML), typically fatal within five days."

Nancy, my wife, and soon to be my caregiver, began to sob and shake uncontrollably. My own feeling that I'd been slammed by a truck was replaced with urgent questions. "Can the MD Anderson doctors save me? What are my chances of survival?" The oncologist calmly replied, "Just go immediately." Apparently, immediate treatment took precedence over my emotional well-being.

Arriving close to midnight, Nancy and I found the emergency room filled to overflowing with suffering, desperate people. We were greeted with the sounds of crying, moaning, deathly coughing, and cries for help. The rooms and halls were saturated with an ominous, depressing atmosphere. Despair overwhelmed me.

An exhausted nurse-receptionist checked us in. She looked at me blankly as I explained that I had been sent there because I had just been diagnosed with AML, and I felt like I was dying. I imagined the nurse thinking, *Oh, another one tonight. Join the club. A doctor will eventually get to you.* Suddenly, a sense of profound isolation and loneliness joined my anxiety and deep despair. I was ushered into my own emergency room, past others suffering on gurneys in the crowded hallway.

Two cancer doctors eventually attended to me. Having seen the results of the blood tests, they began blood infusions immediately and set up the first blood treatment—apheresis, a blood filtration procedure to remove some of the millions of immature white blood cells that were suffocating me by limiting the oxygen-carrying hemoglobin.

In answer to my questions, the doctor said, "If we can get you through the next couple of days, you will have a chance of survival, but less than twenty percent. You must take these pills now, a strong chemo treatment, which will slow the cancer—for now."

"Okay, Doc, thanks for your help. I seldom lose a battle. I will be one of the 20% who survive. How do I achieve that? I will never give up!"

The next morning I awoke in a hospital room. The sun shone through the prison-cell-sized window. I was alive! But I was miserably sick from the chemo treatment and totally alone, seemingly in solitary confinement. Pulling the emergency call cord brought a nurse, who was covered head to toe in sterile white protective garments.

"Good morning, Mr. Cline. You're being isolated in this room for your protection, since you now have no immune system. Your visitors will not be allowed inside the room, but they can talk to you through the phone and from that glassed-in visitors' room."

I was emotionally shattered. Nancy suddenly appeared behind the glass, crying, but forcing a smile for my sake. "Good morning darling. You'll be fine," she said, adding other words of encouragement. It occurred to me that this isolation and Nancy's inability to help when I appeared to be dying would be more difficult for her than for me. So my response was, "I feel good and very alive. I *will* survive and be out of here in no time." When one's life is in the balance, positive encouragement from loved ones and prayers seeking help from the Lord can make the difference between life and death. A positive attitude can be essential to healing.

The month in the hospital was horrific. I lost an average of two pounds a day because of the constant nausea. I became quite weak. Then came hair loss. The athletic, middle-aged, successful environmental engineer had vanished, and in his place was a gaunt, chalk-white, bald old man. With great effort, I began my own, in-room isometric exercises to stave off further atrophy of my muscles.

A cheerful male nurse came in one day, shaved the remaining straggly hair off my head, and presented me with a cute stocking cap, both of which made my day. My brain was lost somewhere in a murky smog from the effects of chemo treatment and the shock of the sudden change in my life. The isolation and lack of human contact were beyond depressing; they felt like punishment. But I wasn't dead. Instead, I was blessed with life, good and caring nurses, very competent doctors, and encouragement from many friends.

Visitors came to wish me well, but they communicated with me from behind the glass. Bill Fowler, a good friend from work, arrived with a poster of bicyclists that had been signed by several hundred friends and associates. Bill asked, "Can I take a picture of you?" I was lying there all dressed up in my sexy hospital gown with injection tubing in my shoulder and oxygen tubes in my nose. "Sure, why not?" I responded, not realizing that the picture would be enlarged and hung in the elevator at work.

The picture was truly an embarrassment when I visited a month later. But it resulted in over 35 pints of blood being donated for me during the next blood drive at work, a good thing for all. Giving blood for a friend and associate in serious trouble is satisfying and leads to happiness for the donor.

My Christian friends Tim and Kathy Coble visited several times, and with their prayers for me, gave me hope. Then a dear friend from Norway, Karl Ole, appeared quite unexpectedly. He looked through the protective glass that separated us and saw an unrecognizable, very old man asleep in the room marked with my name. He found a nurse and exclaimed, "That's not my friend Jeff! Can we find the room he's in?" The nurse insisted that it *was* my room and the patient was me. So Karl Ole re-entered the room and called the old man, using the phone. At that point I awoke and shocked him by responding, "Hello Karl Ole, good to see you." This was a special and uplifting visit, for me at least. These positive and often prayerful visits from loving friends gave me energy, hope, and a determination to survive.

Even though I was an emotional mess and still seriously sick, but no longer losing weight, I was discharged and wheeled out of the hospital in a month. Unobservable inside the sickly-looking old man in a wheelchair was a determination to beat this beast occupying his body, and a happiness to be going home alive, able to be with friends and family again. Those loving friends and our shared faith profoundly influenced my survival. It helped that I had a strong spirit that would not give up—ever, but one should not underestimate the great power of positive, loving, supportive people, believers in life.

This was just the first of many emergency room visits and stays in the hospital that I came to call "Hotel California." I had just begun a journey into a deep darkness from which I would finally emerge several years later, a changed person, both emotionally and physically. Life's journey consists of darkness (difficulties, failures, extreme losses) and light (opportunities, successes, loving relationships). The outcomes depend upon your response. When you are knocked down, don't stay down. Get up and fight. Refuse to dwell on your misery, despair, anger, and self-pity. Make the decision to recover and grow toward the light; form deep friendships, seek to help others, love your neighbor as yourself, and become a positive influence in society.

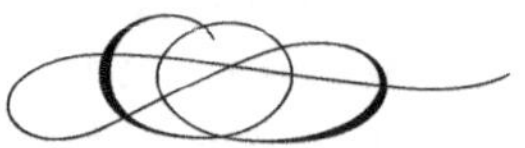

Chapter 2
The Good Life

Prior to the cancer diagnosis, Nancy and I were living the good life. We were empty nesters. Our children, Jamie and Megan, were in college or tech school, developing their talents into potential careers. My professional life was at its zenith, and I loved it, while Nancy enjoyed her career teaching high school math. My excellent health allowed me to be active in many sports and to enjoy active adventure vacations with Nancy in the U.S. and abroad. My highest priorities were work, travel, family, and finally, God. My motto in life, which I tried to live by, was "Travel when possible, work hard, play hard, stay fit, never stop learning, love always, stay loyal, be honest, stay humble, be kind, smile often."

I started work in the upstream oil industry by doing research on enhanced oil recovery and drilling mud systems. As the Environmental Protection Agency began to regulate the upstream industry in the 1980s, my role altered to environmental scientist, since I had been a professor of Environmental Science at Wilkes College (now Wilkes University) years before.

During the five years before the AML cancer, my position as environmental manager and then as water manager at a mid-sized oil and gas company in Houston gave me the opportunity to be a major contributor to producing energy from oil and gas at the lowest possible environmental impact. I was known in the international oil industry's environmental community, developing and publishing papers on water and drill waste treatment systems, developing company environmental programs and strategies, and helping operations to comply with environmental standards. This was a dream-come-true career and personal opportunity for me, finally at the peak of my life's goals.

The downside of working in the upstream oil industry was the high level of stress. While it was exciting, with good pay and benefits, the risk factors were substantial. Layoffs occurred often due to (a) a drop in oil and gas prices, (b) a change in upper management to make the company more "lean and mean," (c) large-scale trading and/or selling of properties, and (d) company mergers. When manpower cuts loomed, the company could be quite an unpleasant place to work. During these layoffs, I typically experienced anxiety, losses (good friends, responsibilities), fear, hurt, disappointments, and betrayals by "friends."

Pursuing fitness helped me to handle the stress. The company gym provided convenient opportunities for daily exercise during a flexible workday, plus the location was surrounded by trails for jogging and bicycling. With weekend workouts of long runs and long-distance, high-intensity group bicycle rides, my fitness level was excellent. My exercise regimen was coupled with a goal of healthy eating. We followed a Mediterranean diet in preparing meals at home. We ate out two to four times a week, which is inherently unhealthy, but in general, we had the health and physical stamina for an active life.

I enthusiastically pursued many sports: skiing, triathlons, footraces, bicycle races, and hiking and climbing in the mountains. In the early years I won awards in both cross-country and downhill skiing, triathlons, bicycle racing, and footraces. During the five years preceding the AML cancer, these activities became more about pleasure than about competition. For example, my high level of fitness allowed me to participate in an annual weekend fundraising event for MS, bicycling from Houston to Austin. I typically raised around $2,000 from contributions of friends and acquaintances for such events. Nancy and I also pursued our love of nature and outdoor sports by taking annual vacations hiking, scrambling, and climbing in the mountains of the American West, Canada, Europe, and South America.

Our family life was limited during that time. Our families lived in Wisconsin and we lived in Houston. My parents would visit once a year on their "snowbird" drive from Tucson to Wisconsin. Occasionally we flew to Wisconsin to attend weddings or graduations, and to visit parents, siblings, nieces, nephews and cousins. So, our friends from work, our neighbors, and our fellow sports enthusiasts became like family to us. Megan and Jamie were pursuing their lives in college, and, regrettably, we weren't able to spend much quality time with them.

We traveled as much as time permitted. We satisfied our love of history and of different cultures with travels to Europe, Costa Rica, Peru, Indonesia, and Canada, usually staying in B & Bs and driving to points of interest. In Peru, we hiked the Inca Trail over several spectacular mountain passes to the ancient Inca sacred city of Machu Pichu. Son Jamie joined us during spring break in a Colorado hiking adventure, ascending 10 mountains over 14,000 feet in elevation. He also joined us, as his graduation present, for a tour of France, in which we visited sites from the Louvre to magnificent cathedrals and palaces, while also cheering on Americans in several stages of the Tour de France bicycle race. Additionally, I traveled to 33 different countries to my company's international locations.

Our last international venture was to Italy, an art and history wonderland. That was where I began to struggle as my health mysteriously declined. I was very tired, losing weight, and I had no appetite. In about four months we determined the cause—undiagnosed cancer.

With the unexpected blow of the cancer diagnosis, my seemingly "good life" was abruptly altered to a struggle for survival, prayers for recovery, and ultimately, a new set of priorities that made life worth living and led to a true and deeper happiness.

Chapter 3
Recovery

Recovery from cancer is not typically a straightforward progression. Rather, as in my case, it is a roller coaster ride up steep hills and down into dark valleys. Serious physical and emotional issues can occur, causing a downward spiral, perhaps even to a death not directly from the cancer. The continued chemo treatments, medication side effects, and ailments like pneumonia from the depressed immune system can strike at any time. And of course, the AML cancer, now theoretically in remission, can reoccur at any time.

My outpatient chemotherapy began the month after initial treatment and release from MD Anderson. The chemo liquids were pumped into my bloodstream from a bag strapped around my waist. The physical effects were relatively minor compared to my severe reaction to the high-dose chemo in the hospital. However, social interactions were compromised. People were curious, even judgmental. At times it was embarrassing, and I did not want to explain the situation. There will always be suffering, and everyone goes through it. I did not want to be defined by my suffering or my treatment. Additionally, my immune system was quite depressed, so I had to avoid crowds, touching or being touched, and anyone coughing. The monthly chemo treatments continued for four months, at which time an appointment was set up to meet with a new doctor, Dr. Jones, to discuss alternative treatments.

Dr. Jones, a bone marrow transplant specialist, discussed the future with Nancy and me. There were two basic approaches to eliminating the leukemia long term: continue taking monthly chemo treatments for an extended period, or kill and replace the bone marrow stem cells containing the defective DNA causing the blood cancer.

Dr Jones recommended that we kill the defective stem cells and replace them with healthy stem cells from a donor. The bone marrow stem cells produce the red blood cells and hemoglobin for delivering oxygen to the body, platelets to prevent bleeding, and white blood cells to fight disease and infection.

In my bone marrow, the stem cell DNA had become defective, resulting in the production of so many immature white blood cells that there were no longer enough red blood cells and hemoglobin to keep me from, in essence, suffocating. The current chemo treatments and blood transfusions were keeping the AML in remission, but with less than a 20% chance of a long-term cure. Dr. Jones recommended the stem cell transplant as soon as possible, before I became weaker, when there would be less chance of surviving the transplant. Either option was a high risk, no matter which of the two paths we chose. We were terrified of either choice, but ultimately decided upon the stem cell transplant after five chemo treatments and four months after my initial hospitalization.

A donor of healthy stem cells that matched my blood characteristics was found. It appeared to be a perfect match, with 12 of 12 parameters matching. My father flew to Houston from Wisconsin to be with me as I was about to get the transplant. He was distressed when I picked him up at the airport, and he began to cry when he saw his hairless, gaunt, pale son. At the hospital Dad maintained a positive attitude with Dr. Jones, assuring him that he was a very good doctor and that he knew he would save his son's life.

A young lady entered my hospital room as I was being prepared for the stem cell transplant. She introduced herself as Ann, a manager at my workplace; she was on the Leukemia and Lymphoma Society's Team in Training. She told me she wanted to compete in the San Diego marathon in my honor. "Would you agree to that?" she asked warmly. "It will be my first marathon."

She wanted to honor me? A complete stranger was giving her precious time and energy to raise money for LLS in a grueling marathon, in my honor? Was she an angel? "Yes," I replied enthusiastically, smiling broadly. This act of love, kindness, and support from a previously unknown young woman, who would become a friend for life, was a powerful, positive emotional uplift. It gave me another reason to live through what was to become a life-challenging ordeal.

Ann returned in a month, while I was still recovering in the hospital, bringing me her marathon hat and medal. She said, "It was so difficult that I could not have done it without your inspiration. I am so happy to have completed my first marathon, and in your honor." Her engaging enthusiasm and positive attitude filled both of us with upbeat energy and peace; she became a light to me and others, demonstrating a key to happiness: reaching out to mentor and support people who need help.

The first step in the transplant procedure was to inject a highly toxic chemical substance that would kill all of the defective stem cells in my bone marrow, hopefully not killing the patient in the process. Calculations by Dr Jones, assuming that I was a "tough guy," resulted in a dosage of 125% to be sure that all the defective stem cells were destroyed. The next day I awoke so sick, that I wondered if this was the end. Nancy had stayed by my side all night on a makeshift couch bed, providing support. She offered to order breakfast, which, with my severe nausea, was repulsive.

The stem cells extracted from my donor were slowly injected into an artery over several hours. The stem cells swam into my bone marrow, where they slowly began to produce healthy white and red blood cells and platelets. Meanwhile, the blood transfusions were now of type B+ blood, rather than my previous type AB+. Donors at my workplace and young adults at the high school where Nancy was teaching donated over 30 pints of blood each. Support from friends is an essential part of survival. One must be "good with friends" (loving, forgiving, supporting) during a severe crisis. One must also be good with the Lord, as life can end in an instant, when it is too late to ask for forgiveness or spiritual help.

The hospital environment was quite difficult for me and everyone else on my floor. The nurses and staff were friendly and helpful, but I was regularly disturbed as I was monitored day and night. This included being stuck with a needle for blood samples at least every four hours. The other patients on the floor were at various stages of the same treatment. All of us were quite sick, and our families were stressed. Many doctors and nurses with different specialties did evaluations and discussed issues in order to determine needs for medications and treatments. The doctor in charge, with his team, left orders, which typically included daily exercise and a request to try to eat and drink more. He also left clarification of medications and instructions for tests to be run and specific monitoring to be done. He or she might also offer encouragement, but that task was usually left to the nurses.

We transplant patients suffer severe reactions to the chemotherapy, to the blood that is new to our bodies, and to the treatment medications. For example, stem cell transplant recipients receive a medication that inhibits their immune system reactions, thereby helping their bodies accept the foreign blood being infused, as well as the foreign blood slowly being generated by the transplanted donor stem cells. Severe reactions are frequent, with life-threatening impacts on all organs. The degenerated immune system provides an opportunity for infection by diseases like pneumonia. Transplant recipients are all quite sick, and many who are weak of body and/or spirit die in the hospital or shortly after returning home. All are extremely exhausted. Nausea makes the consumption of solid food difficult. I began losing about two pounds per day.

My mornings began with seeing daylight and thanking the Lord for giving me another day of life. Then I would greet the new shift nurse, take a shower, and follow that with exercise. Walking while wheeling the pole containing my ongoing infusion bags was difficult in the crowded and instrument-cluttered hallways. But daily exercise was essential—doctor's orders. Nancy brought in my bicycle and exercise rollers so that I could exercise in my room unhindered. This was extremely difficult, but I believed it was necessary for survival. My years of training for ski races and triathlons, and surviving—even thriving—in grueling, long-distance events, were paying dividends now with physical and emotional strength. I was determined not to give up, as I visualized that my sweating on the bicycle was getting the poisons out of my system.

The nurses began stopping by to observe in amazement something never seen before. They were in awe, inspired. My doctor was impressed and saw an opportunity for help with his other patients on the floor, some of whom would not get out of bed and were dying. Dr. Jones asked, "Would you talk to the other patients about getting out of bed to exercise? They will listen to you, since you are sick just like they are. If they do not exercise, they will get pneumonia or have other health problems that will diminish their chances of survival." "Yes, I would be happy to do that," I replied. I began visiting others on the floor to inspire them to get out of bed, to live for their families.

A young man two rooms from me had just died. He had never gotten out of bed after his transplant. A middle-aged woman from Peru, with a husband and three young children, was too sick to get out of bed. "You must get out of bed to exercise at least twice a day. Your children need you. I am very nauseated too, but I carry a pan along to avoid messes in the halls while exercising. You can do it. Do not give in to the exhaustion and the nausea. Just get up, and never ever give up. You must live for your children." She began exercising, survived, and is a cancer-free happy mother today.

I continued on, encouraging others to just get up, get out of bed, and exercise. Although we were being attended to by excellent medical professionals, exercise is one of the six best doctors, the others being sunshine, water, rest, air, and diet.[1] While we could not leave the hospital floor to go outside and enjoy some sunshine, we could all get up and walk or be wheeled to a picture window, looking out upon flower gardens basking in sunshine, a welcome substitute. Helping the other patients was rewarding to me and gave me joy.

The hospital experience for the caregiver is equally challenging. The emotional stress of caring for their suffering and possibly dying loved one is severe. There were

---

1. From a nursery rhyme quoted by Wayne Fields in *What the River Knows*, University of Chicago Press; 1st edition (April 1, 1996)

no beds for sleeping. The caregiver must monitor the medications and treatments and perform care when the nurse is with other patients. The caregiver strives at all times to present a positive, optimistic attitude, so essential to helping a seriously sick person survive and heal. Meanwhile, Nancy was teaching high school mathematics full time as well. The commute from home to the Medical Center was 1 ½ hours through harrowing Houston traffic.

My caregiver, Nancy, was an angel, a very stressed angel. Recently, I asked her, "How did you manage the extreme stress in the five years that I was so sick? This was a deep, deep low for you as well as for me. You had a full-time teaching job, managed the household, and cared for me at home and in the hospital."

With a look of anguish, Nancy said, "I prayed a lot. The Lord gave me emotional strength, helped me to relax, and gave me hope. I walked four to six miles every day for relaxation. I slept very little—about five hours a night during the teaching week. Since we had no family nearby, I frequently talked to my mother and other family members on the phone. And our church family helped; people like Richard Study and others who drove you to MD Anderson Clinics when you were unable to drive and I had teaching obligations. All of the family and friends who helped us provided essential contributions: visits, cards, and calls. They helped me to be positive, bringing love, solace, encouragement and prayers. They all were essential for both of us, for your physical survival, for my emotional survival, and, together, for our well-being."

Nancy and my friends helped me be as at peace as possible so my body could heal itself. They brought me beautiful music (classics, love songs), books on tape, and get-well cards. Nancy insisted that I not watch the news or any negative shows on TV. Instead, she brought me a DVD player, and we watched non-violent movies and "chick flicks." Most importantly, friends came to engage in upbeat conversation about good things present and past, usually ending a visit with a prayer of thanksgiving and a hug.

Reflecting upon Nancy's response, I realized that she had true fortitude, the strength of mind and character that enables one to endure pain, affliction, and uncertainty with courage. With fortitude and determination, anything is possible.

She maintained hope throughout our ordeal. To Nancy, a Christian, Pope Francis's definition of hope is apt. "Hope is the virtue of a heart that doesn't lock itself into darkness, that doesn't dwell on the past, does not simply get by in the present, but is able to see a better tomorrow." Since there was always hope fortified with prayer, she and I never gave up, but rather chose hope and happiness. Happiness can help to cure a person physically and emotionally. Finally, the conversation reinforced that we loved each other very much.

After five weeks in MD Anderson, Dr. Jones announced, "You will be released tomorrow. You are still in remission, but there is a potential for Graft vs. Host Disease (GVHD), a condition in which the new blood attacks the body, particularly the organs." He cautioned, "The first 100 days are important. You will need to come daily for blood tests and infusions for the first month, then once a week for blood tests and checkups. You're a tough guy, but you must be totally honest with any symptoms so we can treat them quickly. Your immune system is depressed. Do not visit crowded places like baseball games or airports." We were overjoyed, actually excited, as I was wheeled out of the hospital, very much alive and with my identification band removed. We hoped this was the end of the cancer ordeal. Unfortunately, it was just the beginning. As we left the hospital, Nancy cried out to the nurses, "What if I make a mistake and kill him?" She was going to be responsible for my oral medications—17 pills daily at different intervals! Nancy also had to go through training to flush my port daily and change my dressing every four days while maintaining a sterile environment. A mistake could cause a serious infection or death.

Recovery from the cancer and GVHD was a wild ride of deep lows of sickness, followed by recovery and rebuilding. In my case, the treatment to halt the advance of the acute myeloma leukemia was a toxic chemical that had been used for over 50 years, with no recent advancements. The cancer did go into remission, but all my organs were hurt and vulnerable. My hair continued to fall out. My immune system had deteriorated, providing other diseases an opportunity to invade. To adjust to this, my diet was restricted—no fresh fruit or salads—just thoroughly cooked hospital food. My visitors were required to wear protective hospital coverings. No children under ten were allowed because they were more likely to be disease carriers.

After each release from the hospital, I would again begin rehabilitation. But inevitably some new sickness or crisis would occur. During the five-year roller coaster, I would be brought back to the emergency room and the intensive care unit four times. There was a total of twelve hospital stays, followed by recovery periods in which I worked on rehabilitating my ever-weakening body. My survival of the fourth near-death experience led my neighbors and friends to call me Lazarus. I absolutely refused to give up. Those near-death experiences included the following:

- Near death upon first arrival at emergency room

- Triple pneumonia, requiring living under plastic tent

- Severe heart trauma from treatment, followed by an ablation to stop atrial fibrillation

- Critical electrolytes below requirements for brain/life functioning

An element of recovery from trauma is religion, as recognized by psychiatrists. Two groups prayed for me daily and sent prayer cards signed by each person. I taped the cards to the fireplace and touched them daily, feeling the love and spirit flowing through me, helping me to heal. I believe that through these prayer groups, the Lord played a huge role in my amazing mental and physical resilience, giving me life.

Physical rehabilitation began with taking walks of ever-increasing length with my dear friend Richard. He had been diagnosed with terminal cancer five years before, but he was in remission and still very much alive.

One day Richard asked, "Would you like to take walks with me?"

"Yes, but I am very slow," I said meekly. "I can barely walk out of my yard, and I need walking sticks to stay upright."

Richard's response was firm. "Okay then; I will be over to walk with you at 7:00 in the morning. Be ready."

Arising in the early mornings was a serious challenge, as I was so absolutely exhausted. My skin itched terribly from the GVHD-induced rash, but nevertheless, I would drag my listless, weak body out of bed each morning and get dressed, covering myself completely to avoid sunlight on my skin. Then we would walk. Then I began doing calisthenics at the end of each walk. The walks increased to over two miles. Richard talked and talked as we walked. He had been a high school teacher and basketball coach, so we talked basketball often, but religion and politics were topics as well. Even though the distance and speed of the walks were ever increasing, the distractions of fun and interesting discussions made the walks seem short. My health and well-being improved. When I could not walk, but instead had to go to MD Anderson or a clinic, Richard drove me there. He was an angel, my guardian angel, and our close friendship grew even more.

Rehabilitation of my muscles and ligaments began with Val, a professional trainer and physical therapist. She had a set of workout equipment at her house. Nancy drove me to my first visit as I was unable to drive and needed assistance to struggle up the short walk to the front door. Upon my arrival, Val and I interviewed each other. She had never had a client who was a cancer survivor or anyone in such a debilitated state of physical health. The first workout was memorable, as I needed assistance to get down and up from the floor mat. Nancy, the caregiver and protector, watched over Val critically. By the end of the test session, I had done several pushups and worked with the lightest bands. Val said, "I can help you to rebuild, if you follow my training regimen, which includes diet. We'll need to work out together twice a week, and you will need to work out in your own gym at least once a week. Here's a recipe for a bodybuilder's smoothie. Make one for yourself daily, and be sure to have one right after a weightlifting session."

And so rehabilitation began. I said, "Val, I am determined to rebuild enough to be able to at least hike in the mountains again and to enjoy sporting activities like bicycling. And I want to have the strength to survive any more health crises."

After a month, I drove myself to Val's gym. She took monitoring measurements and pictures. After six months I was pushing heavy weights, pleasing Val with the definition in re-emerging biceps and quadriceps. At eight months Val took pictures of me after goading me into donning weightlifter garb and striking a bodybuilder pose. She was so pleased and proud of me, now her "favorite, most improved student ever," she beamed. My weight had gone up from a gaunt 142 pounds of sagging skin and bones to 165 pounds, with my body fat remaining at 14%—over 20 pounds of muscle gain! Drooping skin from my once muscular 195-pound body was filling in with defined muscle. I could now do burpees and jump rope. We inspired each other! She encouraged me, helping me to have good, useful workouts even when I was tired or having one of those bad days that many of us cancer survivors suffer. My rapid progress gave Val such joy. Then the initial stages of another near-death experience began, and the rebuilding was suddenly halted.

Triple Pneumonia

John, my good friend, was in the lobby checking in when I arrived at the San Antonio hotel where the technical conference was being held. We were both presenting authors. I had just arrived from Houston, a three-hour drive, during which I had become increasingly ill. During check-in I began feeling weak. "John, could you help me take my bag to my room?" I asked. John said graciously, "Be glad to." John knew of my recent health issues with cancer and was disturbed by my pale face. As I tried to put the card into the lock of my room, my hand began to tremble uncontrollably. "John, can you open the door for me?" I asked. He looked worried and quickly opened the door to my room. I immediately lay down on the bed to recover before going to dinner.

I slept through dinner, the evening, and the night, awaking the next morning only an hour before my presentation. Could I manage to give the presentation, I wondered? Could John give it for me? With trepidation and poor delivery, I met the obligation to present the paper, which had been requested by the session chairperson. The next morning I drove home to Houston. I have no memory of most of the drive.

After I got home Richard drove me to the MD Anderson emergency room. Tests indicated that I had pneumonia, and I was admitted to the hospital. Treatment with antibiotics began immediately. Three days later, when Dr. Jones visited, I felt considerably better. "Dr. Jones, I feel good again. Please release me," I pleaded. "No, Jeff, we can't release you yet. We need to monitor you for at least another day." The next morning I awoke feeling sicker than when I had entered the hospital. More tests were taken, including a lung biopsy.

Nancy was present when Dr. Jones summed up my dire situation. "You have triple pneumonia: bacterial, fungal and viral. This is very serious. You will be moved to a room with controlled ventilation and will need to remain under a plastic tent to avoid any further contamination. Obviously, you don't have a working immune system. We'll be enhancing your immune system with an experimental treatment. The air inside the tent will be regularly treated to combat the viral infection. We really cannot cure the fungal infection, but we will attempt to control it."

Nancy was visibly shaken. My confidence in survival melted away. Damn! I felt so dreadfully sick! Was this the end? Would I ever see my children or good friends again? A foreboding loneliness and dread overcame me. "Lord help me," I prayed. Nancy began to cry quietly.

A month later, Dr. Jones allowed the tent to be removed, explaining, "You are sure one tough guy. We thought you might not make it, but the bacterial and viral pneumonia are cleared up, and the fungal pneumonia is kind of encapsulated. Your immune system is not normal, but it's much improved and will slowly recover. I'll release you tomorrow. But, because of your poor immune system right now, you must avoid all crowds, sick people, children, restaurants, zoos, farms, and gardening, because you would be touching or breathing soil particles and foods that have touched the ground, like strawberries.

"Yes sir!" I exclaimed. "Whatever is necessary to be alive, to not get that sick again." I had survived another near-death experience.

Release from the hospital was glorious. Nancy and I hugged for an eternity after that long month of isolation in the plastic tent. The sun was shining. The trees and flowers were all so beautiful. I was alive, happy, and going home, soon to see friends and family. I exclaimed, "Nancy this is a really good day, and every day, as long as I have life, will be a good day."

After such a close call with death, one's perspective changes; I was so happy just to be alive. Fighting cancer and the related illnesses showed me how fragile life is and therefore, how precious life is. During the long ordeal, the afflicted person faces incredible pain, sickness, exhaustion, anxiety, loneliness, despair, and helplessness. The essential antidote is hope, hope for a better life in the future. I felt boundless gratitude for the support of the hospital staff, my friends, my family, and the Lord. And I realized that I had to live to the fullest while I could and appreciate every day as a good day.

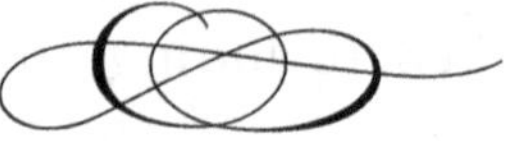

Chapter 4
Getting Back on Track

I was recovering from the cancer and the related side effects and diseases, but I was significantly changed physically and emotionally. I was a new person with new challenges—and new opportunities! Having "chemo brain," I could no longer work in the high-pressure oil industry with its travel demands, nor could I do sporting events. The next important step was to determine what I could do for the rest of my life that would be fulfilling. The actress Mary Pickford wrote, "You may have a fresh start any moment you choose, for this thing we call failure is not the falling down, but the staying down."

My old bicycling buddy, James, offered to mentor me in developing new goals in life. We had ridden together often, helping each other, and having fun. We had ridden numerous MS150s, charity rides from Houston to Austin to raise money for multiple sclerosis research. The riding stopped for me when the AML struck. James called one Sunday afternoon about three years after my original treatment and remission. "Can I come over to visit for a while?" he asked. He arrived with a book, *The Purpose Driven Life* by Rick Warren, and a pad of paper.

James' motive, I later discovered, was to help me seek and pursue a positive purpose in life. I no longer could manage high-stress environments full time; I didn't have the necessary physical or mental stamina. Plus, I hadn't been able to work during the past three years because of the recurring serious medical challenges. However, I had learned that no matter how restricted one is as a result of an unfortunate event like cancer, one can make a choice of how they will respond to that event.

"Jeff, you need to understand yourself. You need to like yourself, to take charge, and pursue your destiny with enthusiasm," James said. "You have a new destiny now, an opportunity to pursue something greater than making some oil executive rich. The Lord has a plan for you, and that is why he allowed you to live. You've got to get off the couch and use your many talents to pursue your God-given destiny."

"But James, many of my talents and special abilities are now hampered. I'm only a skeleton of what I was before the debilitation of the cancer."

James was so patient. "Jeff, you have to quit dwelling on the past. Instead, let's work to discover who you are now so you can just get up and move positively ahead. Read this book by Rick Warren, and we'll discuss each chapter. You know, Jeff, you are an incredible person—so brave, strong, loving, kind, and intelligent. You once amazed me with your bicycling capabilities, but that was yesterday. Now, you inspire many people with your ability to not just survive against all odds, but to recover and help others. You are a blessing. You have hope and an incredible inner strength. You can now retire into doing the work that the Lord has for you. I will be disappointed if you live in the past as a victim. This book will help you discover yourself and God's plan for you. Read it, and if it's all right with you, I'd like to come back next Sunday to discuss it with you."

James continued to visit me every Sunday afternoon for two months. These sessions were difficult and exhausting. There were no magic words coming to me in a dream or a vision that spelled out my new destiny. I set forth an idea of applying my extensive experience in water treatment and management to helping those in need of potable water, particularly in third world countries. But how? I could not even travel by air in my own country without getting sick. How would I survive a third world environment? I wouldn't. James said, "How about working with a U.S.-based consulting company and not traveling? Just staying home doing design and support?" This seemed like a workable idea in theory, but I would have to function reliably at a high level at least five days a week. There were still too many bad days and mandated hospital visits during the week. At the end of our discussions, I decided to set up a water management consulting company in which I could determine the commitments myself.

Because I loved exploring different cultures and hiking in the mountains, I considered these as worthy goals going forward, even though these activities were presently far beyond my altered physical abilities. Could I strive for these as long-term goals? Could I succeed in regaining the ability to again enjoy these activities? In discussions with James, I established both of these activities as goals that I was determined to achieve. Challenge on! It would be necessary to rebuild my body: my immune system, my mental capacity, my circulatory/blood system, and most organs, especially my heart, skeletal, and muscular system.

Another goal was to help others as much as I was able. I began to support charity groups at my church and to mentor youths at two schools. I began supporting several consulting firms and companies related to the oil industry, helping with environmental and water management issues. Helping others took my focus away from myself. Helping others gave me purpose, pride, and joy.

James helped me to re-establish positive life goals, a critical step to recovery. He helped me to take charge of my life and enthusiastically accept my new-found destiny. We agreed that I was the only one who could determine what I wanted to be, what I wanted to do, what I wanted to have. I was the only one who could determine what would truly bring me satisfaction and a sense of fulfillment.

It was James who had referred me to Val, the professional trainer and physical therapist mentioned in Chapter 3. She had never worked with a determined cancer survivor, let alone one with a goal to again hike in the mountains. She prepared me to enjoy hiking at altitude and to be prepared to survive through any future serious illnesses resulting from the GVHD response. My hope for a better life and achieving my goals grew. Recovery through exercise was ultimately a successful journey from wheelchair to climbing mountains again. (And there are still many more mountains to climb).

Nancy and I joined a church and a bible study group called the Empty Nesters. I also joined a Christian men's group. These groups helped satisfy our need for positive support during recovery from a tragedy. We enjoyed socializing and doing charity work together. From these groups emerged some strong, loving relationships as well as positive, useful mentoring during times of stress.

I began teaching a course, "Energy and the Environment," at the nearby community college. Considerable preparation was necessary to learn the details of each energy-producing technology, including those under development. The environmental effects of each were determined semi-quantitatively. Costs, financial and environmental, were estimated and compared relatively. This process helped my brain to rebuild while teaching students about the environmental effects of energy generated from each source.

The chemotherapy had caused what the doctors called "chemo brain." Concentration, memory, and executive function were seriously depressed. The good news is that the brain functions can be recovered with a healthy diet, daily aerobic exercise, and regular mental exercise. Nevertheless, at this point of recovery, Nancy made all the financial decisions and paid the bills. She and our friends also acted as my chauffeurs until I was mentally able to safely manage driving among the aggressive Houston drivers. Ego adjustments were necessary. I had to focus on the mental and physical recovery possible until full recovery resulted in good, logical decisions.

Either Richard or Nancy continued to walk with me daily. As my physical ability improved, so did my emotions and my overall health. Exercise with friends, especially outside in nature, satisfies several of the "doctors" in Wayne Field's list in *What the River Knows*: exercise, sunshine, and positive socializing.

Another Near-Death Experience

Such severe tiredness overcame me that getting out of bed was nearly impossible. My speech first became slurred and then incomprehensible. I did not feel well. Nancy took me back to the hospital. Tests indicated pneumonia and extremely low sodium and potassium levels. Doctor after doctor visited to no avail until an endocrinologist finally found and fixed the problem. My sodium and potassium levels had dropped to a level at which only one person in the world was documented to have survived.

Sodium and potassium ions are essential for brain function. The endocrinologist discovered that there was no adrenalin in my system. My adrenal glands had shut down. Without adrenalin, the body "wastes" sodium and potassium, and the immune system shuts down.

The brain works through electrical messaging, for the most part through these sodium and potassium ions. Without them motor functions and speech become more and more depressed, ultimately resulting in death. I was given adrenalin, sodium, and potassium through an IV. By the next day, I was walking and able to talk again. Two days later, Dr. Jones released me from the hospital again. Shaking his head he said, "Your situation was discussed at our group meeting. Not a single doctor had ever heard of this illness—GVHD causing the adrenal glands to stop functioning. You really are a tough guy. Your survival is unbelievable." Yes indeed. I had experienced a miracle. I had survived the fourth near death experience in a span of five years.

The roller coaster ride continued. I had worked to rebuild, only to again be admitted to the hospital from a GVHD-related issue. My ambitions and goals remained the same. About five years after the original diagnosis of leukemia, this treatment and remission was the end of serious illnesses resulting from GVHD (Graft versus Host Disease) caused by the stem cell transplant. Each hospitalization left me weaker, but I never lost hope. Positive recovery resulted each time by always moving toward the light in the darkness.

I now keep bees. Bees illustrate the power of working together as one, showing that all things are possible, even surviving cancer.

As I recovered, I did not retire into inactivity. I set new life goals that were seemingly impossible under the circumstances. My goals became achievable by focusing on joy, maintaining a positive attitude, and by never giving up. My advice: avoid despair no matter how dire your circumstances seem. Cultivate hope. Live life with a purpose. Help others, make new acquaintances, learn from your past experiences, and apply what you've learned to become a better person. Be positive, happy, and filled with joy.

You are the only one who can determine what you want to be, what will truly bring you satisfaction and a sense of fulfillment. Practice introspection. What do you believe to be true? What do you perceive as your unique talents, abilities, skills, personality traits, and aptitudes? Your value is an expression of what you love and what you believe is most worthy of love. Your destiny is your purpose for living, which only you can define. Once you define it—and you must, to make life worth living—then enthusiastically pursue your destiny.

My life continues to have purpose—serving God and family and using the gifts and abilities the Lord has given me.

God intervened to save me so that I could fulfill his purposes, his greater destiny for me. Possibly this is true for you as well.

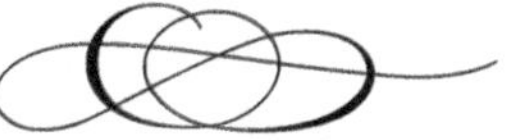

Chapter 5

A Renewed Life

As Nancy and I are sitting outside our cottage along the Colorado River in a beautiful mountain valley between towering "fourteeners," we are pondering the past eleven years of our lives together, years dominated by our battle to survive my cancer. She had been a key part of my fight for survival—an indispensible, loving, supporting caregiver. She had survived intense emotional stress, including my four near-death events. I had needed a wheelchair at times. Chemo treatments and some of the prescription medications had initially left me with limited memory and executive function. Mentally and emotionally, I had been what Nancy had called a mess.

Now, as we gaze at the majestic mountains, we begin to list our blessings as a way of helping us reflect on who we have become. We have life, loving family and friends, special grandchildren, we can again enjoy traveling to experience different cultures, we have fair health, and we are comfortably retired. We agree that I have emerged emotionally strong, refocused on living life within God's plan to help others. We are hopeful, content, and happy.

Simply put, my focus has become to love my neighbor as myself, thereby avoiding self-centered behavior. I said to Nancy, "I still have the gift of life, the most important thing. The Lord has given me a wake-up call to begin doing what I was put here to accomplish. I know that means to use my personal capabilities and talents to help others. But what exactly is it that I—that we—are supposed to do?"

Nearly a year after this discussion, Pope Francis addressed this question. He appealed to all people to do good to others less fortunate, during a TED presentation to a mostly secular gathering on April 27, 2017. The Pope explained, "When one realizes that life, even in the middle of so many contradictions, is a gift, that love is the source and the meaning of life, how can they withhold their urge to do good to another fellow being?

"With non-stop news reports examining the plight of migrants and refugees, victims of violence, the terminally ill, the unemployed and others for whom life is a daily struggle, it's easy to grow complacent inside the safety of our blessings."

The Pope went on, urging us to realize that we easily could be "one of the discarded people," ourselves, and that this realization should spur us to gratitude, action and outreach."

The Pope's message helped me focus on what I could do specifically. Presently, I am helping others in three different meaningful volunteer activities: mentoring teenagers at the Tulsa Boys Home, writing letters to assist incarcerated people in the G1 Christian Prison Ministry, and helping to raise money as a board member of the Tulsa Leukemia and Lymphoma Society (LLS)." All three are rewarding to me, even though we volunteers aren't often thanked directly nor even informed of our specific successes. Success in mentoring and the prison ministry occurs when the person becomes a productive member of society.

The G1 prison ministry evaluates the reincarceration rate three years after release. Of those who met the requirements and learned two things: self-discipline and to love their neighbors as themselves, only 12% were reincarcerated, versus 72% reincarceration of inmates released from the entire Oklahoma prison system.

The G1 prison ministry holds monthly gatherings of those now in minimum security prisons, along with several released former inmates. All tell their stories. A remarkable young lady explained proudly, "I was convicted and imprisoned three times. I rarely had the opportunity to even see my children. The last time I was imprisoned, I knew that I had to do something different; I had to quit going down this destructive path. I joined the G1 Christian prison ministry, where I learned to love the Lord, love myself, love others, especially my children, and to treat others like I would like to be treated. I was released six months ago. I now have a good job, for which I must leave soon in my own car." Personally, I was so happy for this woman and others like her who were going through a transformation from being a taker to being a giver by becoming a constructive member of society. These stories of personal success are deeply rewarding for all of us participating in the G1 Christian prison ministry.

The teenagers, ages 16 to 18, whom we mentor at the Tulsa Boys Home are placed there by the Department of Corrections. They typically are from homes with drugs, often from single parent homes, or are orphans. They all have suffered traumatic experiences. We are unpaid Christian men, who present to them a normal and wise fatherly friend who cares about them. We encourage them with hope and faith. We watch them grow, mature emotionally, and with joy and satisfaction, occasionally see apparent success stories. These stories may include high school graduation with plans for a career path, which can be further education in college or technical school.

The goal of the Tulsa Leukemia and Lymphoma Society is to annually raise about $300,000. This is used for research to develop enhanced treatments and helping those afflicted in Oklahoma. My dedication to the LLS was triggered one day in an elevator at the MD Anderson hospital, which is attached to the Children's Hospital for Leukemia and Lymphoma. A bald child of about five in a wheelchair was crying. Her distressed mother was handling the wheelchair. Bags of injection fluids were hanging above her and entering a port in her shoulder. This was not fair—a child so young with this terrible cancer. It broke my heart, and I thought, *Lord help me to live through my own affliction, and I will do what I can to help other afflicted people, especially children with blood cancers.* Last year the FDA approved the first cancer treatment method which uses genomics (i.e. it uses a person's own genes to detect and cure the cancer). This treatment breakthrough was developed through a laboratory sponsored by the LLS. Most of the blood cancers have experienced a substantial cure improvement rate and reduced mortality during the eight years I have been associated with the LLS.

All three of these charities help others less fortunate, giving me joy, happiness and pride. Life can be so difficult, but I have many blessings, dear friends, and faith, which are the foundation of my optimistic hope and happiness.

My altered life, filled with abundant blessings, looks very different from what I had imagined twenty years ago.

I'm dedicated to family, especially my grandchildren and to friends, like Karl Ole who supported me so warmly in the early days of my illness.

I'm an engaged Christian with an active church life.

I'm enhancing the environment through gardening and beekeeping and by consulting in water management in the oil industry.

With Nancy, I'm having adventures again. They may be modified, but they are still adventures. We've enjoyed Wyoming, the Boundary Waters Wilderness of Minnesota, Olympic National Park, the San Juan Islands of Washington, Vancouver Island, and New Zealand, to name a few.

I'm bicycling again!

You too can achieve happiness by taking charge of your life and committing to your goals. When I believe that everything that happens in my life is a God-scheduled opportunity, it brightens my outlook and infuses me with a greater sense of purpose and confidence.

Chapter 6
Mentoring Brianna

During a trip to Ireland in the fall of 2017, we connected with Kenneth and Brianna, two very dear Norwegian friends. We had contacted them earlier to let them know we would be in the British Isles for a month. They had used up their vacation time for the year. Nevertheless, they figured out a way to meet us for a weekend in Dublin. Kenneth called and said emphatically, "We are really keen to meet with you two when you visit the British Isles."

Kenneth and I had met when we worked together at Amoco Norway in the early 1990s. We both enjoyed cross-country skiing, fishing, and scuba diving, so he took me diving in the kelp beds of the North Sea, where we speared fish and collected crabs and lobsters for dinner. The water was frigid, the seas rough, and the tides merciless, making the excursions an adventuresome challenge. Kenneth was stronger than I and ensured our survival. We cross-country skied in the mountains for fun and for training. We competed in a 55 km ski race across the mountains, which I somehow completed, though totally exhausted. Kenneth and his wife, Brianna, invited us to their hutte on the sea, where we came to know and bond with them as we ate the seafood we gathered (cod, saithe, and crab), and enjoyed a bit of wine.

Fast forward to 2017. We were meeting for the first time since Kenneth had visited me in Houston when I was dealing with the cancer. On a Friday evening, we all arrived at the designated hotel in downtown Dublin. We had changed our initial lodging arrangements from a castle B & B to a hotel with easy access to the airport. Kenneth and Brianna greeted us with smiles and hugs. During that last visit to Houston, Kenneth had discovered a dying old man—all skin and bones, bald, and so weak that getting out of bed required an aide. He had insisted that this was not the strong, athletic environmental engineer whom he had known. Here we were together again ten years later, but now I have hair, albeit gray hair, and I'm upright and smiling.

Conversation was spontaneous, but there was a certain sadness about Brianna and Kenneth. After we caught up on family news, we decided to go for a walk and possibly have dinner at a nearby pub. Brianna suddenly walked up alongside me, grabbed my arm, looked into my eyes and whispered, "Jeff, I don't feel well. I had a bad fall that caused nerve damage. My muscles hurt all over. I haven't any energy. I feel sick and many days I can't leave the house."

"Have you been to a doctor?" I asked anxiously.

Brianna replied, "Ja, several times, but they cannot find anything wrong with me." Brianna went on, describing more symptoms and testing performed by local doctors. Nancy and Kenneth found a dinner pub with a suitable menu offering. Once seated, Brianna and I continued discussing her serious health dilemma. Norway has socialized medicine, but Brianna did not want to seek or pay for medical help at clinics in England or the United States. Brianna pleaded, "Jeff, you were so sick with leukemia, we all thought you might not survive. But you did. Just look at you! How did you do it? Can you help me to find a way to get better like you did?"

Now, understand that Norwegians are only likely to go to church on special holidays like Easter and Christmas.

I began cautiously giving Brianna an alternative method for helping to heal herself. "Brianna, it is possible to heal yourself, even when doctors are unable. First, allow your body the opportunity to heal by removing stress. Don't listen to the news. Avoid negative people. Eat healthy foods, avoiding sugar as much as possible. Play soothing music often—focus on the classics. Concentrate on loving Kenneth and your daughters.

"Most importantly, realize that loving the Lord can be healing. Pray to the Lord, first thanking him for all of the blessings he has bestowed on you and your family. Then ask the Lord to help you to heal. This is what I and many friends did daily when I was very sick. There is a magical, strong, healing power that comes through prayer from loving friends and family.

"If you believe in the Lord and trust and love him, then anything is possible."

Brianna stared at me in deep thought. There were no questions or comments, and I worried that I had offended her, rather than given her helpful advice. We all ordered dinner with a Guinness and enjoyed the performance of three fiddlers.

Early Sunday morning, Nancy and I flew to Edinburgh, and Kenneth and Brianna flew to Norway. We forwarded Brianna a bible. Since then, Brianna has become an exceedingly happy grandmother. She told me that she is feeling much better, and I hear excitement in her voice when she speaks of her children and grandchild. We inspired each other, each of us gaining joy and happiness.

Chapter 7

Just Get Up

It doesn't matter what the challenge in your life's journey is—health, accidents, academics, sports, relationships, humiliation, money—you will get knocked down. The rule is *just get up*. Angela Kouplen and Amber Young are two women who just got up, dusted themselves off, and tried again.

My Wife, Angela, the Warrior
by Sean Kouplen

In early December, 2016, my wife, Angela, went to the doctor for a routine physical examination. There was really no reason for her to get an exam, except that she would get points toward her company's wellness program and, as the highest-ranking female executive in her publicly traded energy company, she wanted to lead by example.

During her checkup, her doctor noticed something strange in her upper breast. She said it was probably nothing, but Angela should have it checked out. Angela acted immediately and called to request a CT scan and a follow-up appointment with a respected local breast cancer surgeon. During this appointment, the surgeon said it appeared to be cancerous and suggested immediate surgery.

Angela called to give me the news. It was certainly scary, but we were both optimistic because she had found the cancer so early. She quickly went into surgery, which was declared a success. The cancer was limited to one small area, and it had been contained. No cancer had been found in her lymph nodes. The tumor would be sent to the lab for analysis, and we would meet as soon as possible to discuss the findings and future treatment options. It appeared that chemotherapy and radiation could be avoided.

About a week later, we met in the doctor's office to learn that the makeup of the tumor and its rapid growth necessitated more aggressive treatment. The treatment regimen would include 17 chemo treatments and 33 radiation treatments. She would lose her hair, eyelashes, toenails, fingernails, experience nausea, achiness, bloody noses, sores in her mouth, exhaustion, and loss of her taste buds. The news of this radical treatment was very difficult to take.

I will never forget having breakfast with Angela immediately after learning about this treatment. It was a daunting and scary time for both of us, but Angela had tremendous resolve. She was determined to keep our lives as normal as possible and not allow these treatments to change our lives. We agreed that this would be an excellent opportunity for us to show the world that our faith in God was as real during difficult times as it was during good times, and that we weren't only fair-weather Christians.

Angela's 15-month cancer journey was truly remarkable. Despite the tremendous side effects mentioned above, Angela never missed one day of work. That's right—not one day. She learned how to properly hydrate herself with IVs after her treatments and get rest when she could. She decided against a wig and instead matched scarves with her work outfits. She maintained an amazingly positive attitude, kept our household organized, and performed tremendously in her executive role, managing over 80 full-time employees.

It is now May 2018, 17 months after Angela's initial diagnosis. She has some lingering side effects from a chemo drug she must take for five years, but overall, she is doing great. Her hair, eyelashes, fingernails and toenails have grown back and she is more beautiful than ever.

Many have asked me about the source of Angela's strength during this difficult time and I believe there were several. Her faith was clearly the primary source of her strength. Angela has a quiet, but deep faith, and she would start each day in prayer and reading the *Jesus Calling* devotional. We were very public about Angela's cancer journey for one reason and one reason only: to encourage as many people to pray for her as possible. We believe that thousands prayed for her, and we are certain this played a huge role in her amazing mental and physical resilience.

Angela's important role as a wife and mother of three also spurred her on. This amazing woman is so important to our family. She is our cheerleader, coach, and organizer, the lifeblood of our family. I believe she knows this and felt compelled to stay strong, even when she didn't feel like doing so.

Finally, Angela's status as a role model within her company and our community also motivated her. Many women look up to Angela because of her tremendous accomplishments, grace, generosity, and kindness. I believe she felt the importance of being a role model, and it kept her going as well.

My wife has impacted the lives of thousands of people who followed her journey. She is a warrior whose determination and faith in God provide an example for all of us to follow. If you are struggling right now, I hope you will use her example to encourage yourself to have the strength and fortitude to fight hard every single day.

Amber: Doing Time
by Jeff Cline

I met Amber when she gave a presentation at an Operation Hope Christian Prison Ministry fundraiser. A short, dynamic woman, full of energy, she always has a ready smile and a laugh. She had been released from prison six months earlier and was still on parole. Her life had been filled with tragedies, culminating in incarceration, yet she exuded joy, glorying in the blessings she'd had upon release.

Smiling broadly, Amber announced excitedly, "My three-year-old granddaughter said to me on Facebook Messenger just after I was released, 'Nana, you look just like me!' I began crying and laughing at the same time. My greatest dream was coming true. This grandchild had made life worth living when I was in jail. I love her so much. I travel to Muskogee every week to visit and play with her and hug her."

Amber became philosophical. "I lost the opportunity of building a relationship with my daughter during my granddaughter's first three years, because I was in jail for 4½ years, for which I am responsible. I cannot make up those lost years, but I can learn from my past mistakes and build those relationships going forward. You can build forward starting anytime. You can start today.

"I needed to fix myself, to reset my mind. I had to forgive others for what they had done to me. I had to forgive my grandfather for sexually abusing me. At the same time, I had to forgive myself for hurting others. Still today I am making amends. I had to realize that some things, like the sexual abuse, were not my fault. I could hate my grandfather for that abuse, but I could still love him for the grandfatherly good things he did, like taking me fishing. I am still in an interactive counseling class to help me get over the anger and the crying, to just forgive and let go. Jesus teaches us that, but I need help to actually do it. Talking with my two mentors and those in class really helps."

When Amber was released from prison, Operation Hope provided her with the essentials: clothing, a bus pass, job listings, and a backpack with toiletries. She explained, "Most importantly I received a sense of community. Someone cared! They also set up a temporary home for me at a Christian-based halfway house called Exodus House." Amber said with conviction, "I believe everyone being released from prison should live in a halfway house for at least six months to help with the adjustment to life on the outside. Exodus House has programs, counseling sessions, and mentors. They set me up with a church and helped me get a social security number and a driver's license. Transitioning out of prison is overwhelming. Operation Hope and Exodus House have made it smoother and helped me to head in the right direction."

In 1969, Amber was born in Oklahoma City to a family with serious problems. Both parents were alcoholics. Her mother was later diagnosed with paranoid schizophrenia. Amber dealt with it by simply leaving the house at times after she was 12 years old. She was an "Army brat," transferring to different bases in the U.S. as a child and finally to Germany as a teenager. There she suffered the trauma of many nearby random bombings during the time of the fall of the Berlin Wall. Nevertheless, she came to enjoy living in Frankfurt, with its many opportunities. However, she eventually had to return to the U.S. and "small town USA," where she graduated from high school in Canadian, Oklahoma.

Amber left Canadian when she married into the Army at age 18 and moved to a base in California. She started a new life, only to experience several traumatic, broken relationships and divorces through the years. In her first marriage, the abuse began soon after marriage. Even though Amber was pregnant, the two divorced after two tumultuous years. She began college, but after two years, her father attempted suicide. The stress led Amber to quit college.

By 1993 Amber had a steady boyfriend with whom she had her second son in that same year. They married and had a daughter in 1996. Amber said she found Jesus that year." But again, the abuse started and continued and got worse. The divorce ended with her ex-husband's taking the children and keeping them through an ugly custody battle. In 2006 she married for the third time—at Gospel Rescue Mission in Muskogee. With this husband, she had another daughter. After six years, the marriage ended. As the two were contemplating divorce, Amber confessed that the overwhelming stress and anxiety was too much, and she began coping by getting strung out on drugs, primarily methamphetamine.

When a tragedy occurs with a breaking relationship, a person can choose one of three paths: to repair the relationship, move on positively to a better relationship, or spiral down to a dark place with worry, anger, and victimhood. Amber began taking drugs to cope with a declining, then broken relationship, which ultimately led to a broken life.

Amber said emphatically, "Meth is the devil! It began to destroy my body. I could no longer work. I had to sell everything to survive. Soon I was a homeless street person. I had to steal to eat and support the habit. The next step in my downward spiral was inevitable. I got busted! In August of 2012, I was sentenced to twenty years in prison for stealing and drugs." She confessed, "I entered prison strung out on meth. But that was the last meth, the last drug of any kind that I would take. I was so sad at not seeing my children for 20 years. My daughter was pregnant when I was taken into custody. Gut-wrenching remorse and despair set in when I thought I would never see my granddaughter grow up."

Amber began assessing her situation. "How did I get myself into this prison and into this mess?" With self-assessment and the help of counselors, she realized that her life began under very difficult circumstances. She had alcoholic parents. She was abused by her parents and a grandparent. She had followed a pattern by marrying into abusive situations. She said, "I had no energy, no self-esteem, and I was now seriously depressed. I had no friends. And I did not want my family to come to the prison." Amber said with the smile of a warrior, "I decided to not give up, but to change instead." The next step of her self- assessment was accepting and surviving in her new "home" for 20 years. Prison, she discovered quickly, was a morbid, boring place with lousy food. She observed a social order, but proclaimed forcefully, "I refused to be gay, and I decided not to do drugs or associate with the drug group.

"I knew I must find a way to honestly work my way out of this place as quickly as possible, but how? I knew that I had to reset my mind to a positive state. I decided to do whatever was required by the system to have my sentence reduced, to be released earlier than the 20 years. I needed to focus my mind on a reduced sentence, commanding myself to never again do wrong things that would put me back in prison."

Amber began to work in earnest to reset her mind. She became active and engaged in Christian activities. She participated in church services twice a week. She began doing bible studies at the prison and also online. She continued the Christian coursework throughout her incarceration and is still engaged in bible study today.

Her most useful course was "Women of the Word." Her best class was "Shelter from the Storm," a sexual abuse class. Topics included marriage, family, raising children, and improving self-esteem. In the group sessions, there was grief sharing, as well as personal buildup and support. Amber whispered, "I began getting closer to the Lord; I began to realize that God loved me in spite of my past. With the love of God, I began to like and then love myself. As I worked through the teachings in the Bible, I began to understand that I had not been treating others the way I would like to be treated. I did not like it at all when my only belongings were stolen when

I arrived in prison; therefore I should not steal from others." The inspiration in passages in the Bible helped her to refocus her thoughts on the positive: building relationships, deciding to be happy, and having hope. Her self-esteem was growing. She was beginning to smile and laugh occasionally. Her depression was decreasing. She began making friends, even some close friends.

Amber demonstrated an essential initiative by taking courses, eventually taking every class offered at Eddie Warrior women's prison. This would give her credits to reduce her sentence and be released more quickly. Her first course, which she began immediately, was 181 hours of Regimented Substance Abuse Recovery. Amber vowed never to do substance abuse again. Her first test of that vow was in prison, where she refused to take any drugs. "Besides," explained Amber, "if I got caught with drugs in jail, my sentence could actually be increased, and I was determined to do everything I could to be released early." She also took courses that would increase her chances of getting a job after release.

At the prison, Amber got a job as assistant operator of the call center. She explained, "I was like an executive assistant. I also worked in the laundry, did cleaning, and tended flower beds. I also worked with computers. In short, I did whatever I could. The pay was only 50 cents per hour, but it made me feel productive, and it would look good on a resume when I was released. Additionally, I received credits towards early release.

"I never received a single demerit write-up for bad behavior. Every command was followed by a "yes sir." I minded authority. I always asked for permission before doing anything, because in prison you can't ask for forgiveness. Instead, you will get write-ups. My good behavior and attitude was one of the major factors leading to my early release after 4½ years—after having received a 20-year sentence."

Amber's mother died midway through her incarceration. Her mother was the only family member to visit her in jail. A short time later, her father died. She mourned her mother's death, alone in prison. Her depression was almost overwhelming with the loss of her mother. She leaned on supporters from her counseling and bible study groups. Tending the gardens outside helped her cope. "Working outside with nature really gave me peace. It was satisfying, even fulfilling, to plant flowers and watch them grow. I watched a nest with eggs become baby birds, watched the parents push the young birds from the nest one day, and then watched the parents teach them how to find food. By connecting with nature, I was connecting with God. It brought me some respite of peace from the stress of losing my mother. It was a temporary escape from the awfulness of prison." Amber grinned and chuckled. "I learned a lot about life from watching those birds and growing the garden." She lit up, becoming happier by just talking about those special moments connecting with nature while she was incarcerated.

"Did many others follow your lead to substantially reduce their sentence while incarcerated?" I asked. "No," she replied. "Most people don't want to get their shit together; they just want to get out. They'd rather spend their days watching TV or sitting on their bed doing nothing. I was being as productive as I could: working, going to classes, reading the Bible and other books. Those who do nothing to improve themselves don't change; they don't rehabilitate. They may get released, but they're back in jail in a short time. People have to get off their butts. I've changed for the better in so many positive ways, and therefore I won't go back to prison. Instead, I will be with my grandchildren, work hard at a good job, never take drugs, and I'll be married soon, this time for life!"

"I practiced positive affirmation every day. This helped me reset my mind to achieve my goals. I did this on my own for months. I'd look in the mirror and tell myself over and over how beautiful I was, how good, how intelligent, how kind. Some girls even started doing the positive reinforcement with me. The positive affirmation made me feel happy, improved my self-esteem, and helped me to feel comfortable in my own skin. Another daily inspiration was reading my daily devotional, *Jesus Calling*. Near the end, I began to read through the Bible on my own, starting at Genesis. I'm now in the Book of John, where Jesus teaches about love." Amber was grinning, actually glowing with joy.

She embellished on her improving attitude and self-image. "Bible studies, bible reading, and church services all contributed to my eventually having hope while I was inside. I could finally begin to see a better future. I was emerging from the deepest darkness into the light. I could envision playing with my grandchild. I let go of dark things. I began having better dreams and a better understanding of myself and life. I hoped to reconnect with family, as none were visiting me. I wrote them letters, especially to my daughter and granddaughter, but I never heard back," Amber mourned.

"Amber, what are your goals and aspirations, now that you are out of prison?" I queried. She responded excitedly, "Operation Hope helped me, gave me clothes, basic necessities, and transportation. Now I have a good job with Operation Hope as an administrative assistant intern. They are my community. I've gotten my driver's license and my own car. I have glasses, new teeth, and health insurance. And best of all, I have a computer, so I can talk to my granddaughter each day and hear her say, "Nana, you look just like me!" I've only been out of prison seven months, and I'm wearing an ankle bracelet because I'm on parole until next February. I must make the transition slow so I don't make serious mistakes.

"To really love my family going forward, I must forgive others and forgive myself, as Jesus taught. I am making amends right now. I recommend that everyone do the grieving and forgiveness classes to help get past the anger, resentment, victimhood, and crying. I am teaching my daughter what I have learned. Also, I recommend for those nearing release to take the life skills class. It helps you to know what to do and what to look forward to on the outside of those gray walls. The class covers everything from finances and finding a job to finding a home.

"Operation Hope helped me be accepted into Exodus House. I now attend services at three different United Methodist churches. My fiancé is a member of one of these. We will not get married until I am off parole. He is my hero. He stuck with me throughout my incarceration. My mentors have warned me not to not go back to the old places, bars and such, and to the friends who were bad influences on me. They work with me daily to continue to reset myself to a life of doing the right things, to be a positive part of society, rather than a negative element. The right thing might be to avoid staying out late when the temptations and circumstances might lead to trouble. This transition is overwhelming at times, but my mentors and church family are a positive support system that helps me, so that I will not ever go back to prison.

"I'm still working through my goals: contact and get together with my children, save money, acquire and keep a good job, make amends with people whom I have hurt, enjoy being with and loving my grandchildren. I would like to help others. Perhaps I could help in a Christian Prison Ministry in a function or program that no one else has yet developed. I am still searching for where God is calling me to help. I will continue to love and listen to the Lord. I must dedicate myself right now to my own self-improvement. Just understand Mr. Cline, I feel so much joy inside, I'm so happy; I'm so blessed, and I have unbelievable hope in the future."

In Amber's life journey, the time in prison was the beginning, rather than the end. She chose to just get up after being knocked down, to be rehabilitated, and to seek a better life. While incarcerated, she moved ahead aggressively and positively in the following ways:

Establishing a self-improvement strategy, including group counseling, to reset her mind.

- Avoiding drugs.

- Taking courses to reduce her sentence and learn valuable skills.

- Participating in Christian activities, including bible studies and church services, which can also reduce a sentence.

- Working in the prison to earn money and help build a resume.

- Respecting authority—never receiving a demerit write-up.

Amber chose to take responsibility for her past actions and work to become rehabilitated. Today, she is realizing her dream of playing with her granddaughter and building a relationship with her. She has a job she likes, a car, a church family, and a community of caring friends. She continues to transition cautiously through the following strategies:

- Living in a Christian-based halfway house.

- Avoiding the places and people who were a bad influence in the past.

- Continuing Christian-based activities and self-improvement counseling.

- Forgiving others who had hurt her and forgiving herself.

- Building relationships with family and friends and doing the right thing.

I believe Amber will never go back to prison, but rather will be a positive contributor to our community. She is filled with joy and hope in the future.

The Fall and Rise of Paul

When my phone rang, I recognized the number. It was my old running buddy's wife, Betsy, with alarming news. Her husband, my very dear friend Paul, was in the hospital. He had fallen off a ladder onto a hard concrete floor, gravely injuring both legs and arms. He was in intensive care.

Paul is a quiet, thoughtful, and intelligent chemical engineer. He's tall and muscular, a big man for a marathon runner. As a runner myself, I was very worried. Over a year later, he shared with me the details of his accident and the long journey to his incredible recovery. Here is Paul's story in his own words.

Seventeen months ago, I fell off a ladder onto a concrete floor, shattering my left wrist, breaking my right upper arm, i.e., the humerus, the ball of which fits into the shoulder joint, and incurring a spiral fracture in my left tibia, the main weight-bearing bone of my calf.

The experience changed me, or perhaps it simply exponentially intensified changes that had started well before the accident. Among these changes has been a deeper Christian spirituality, especially one with more appreciation and sensitivity for radical joy, radical love, and radical mercy. I have also become much more extroverted. In short, I am on a journey of healing myself, a journey from which I hope to learn how to help others to heal. I don't know where this journey is taking me, but like my new friends who have gone through similar experiences, I count myself as lucky.

My surgeon originally indicated that whatever level of healing I achieved in about eight months would probably be the most I could get. That seemed roughly correct, but I am continuing to recover, and I am planning on continuing to do so. This requires discipline and planning for nearly daily self-therapy. Having come so far, I would like to share some of the strategies that have helped me and that may help you, the reader.

- **Keep positive.** Staying positive will help you heal because you are more likely be proactive in caring for yourself. My first and most important suggestion in growing a positive attitude is to find or create a support group with other trauma victims. You will have close to instant rapport with them, and they with you. They will understand what you are going through. It is an awesome synergy, with many injured and recovering people helping each other. In fact, I have identified a few different channels for helping others going through difficult times, and I hope to do this for the rest of my life.

- **Listen.** Because I spent a few days completely unable to care for myself and a few more weeks mostly unable to care for myself, I wanted to connect with those around me, mainly my caregivers. So I listened carefully, tried to figure out where they were coming from mentally and what they were trying to do. Then I tried to verbally reflect this back to them, asking questions, and thanking them. I viewed my early therapists as my best friends, and I tried to give 110% for them.

- **Push yourself.** I tried to do all the physical activities I could that were consistent with my disabled state. Usually I exercised for about the first half hour of each day, always pushing the reps, intensity, and duration beyond what the therapists suggested, adding any variations I could think of. Occasionally the therapists told me to back off, which I would usually do for a while. There were no injuries from this, only a faster recovery. My core wasn't injured, so doing bridges was always part of my routine, as well as stiff-leg knee raises, knee bends, and trying to touch each hand's fingers with that hand's thumb. This therapy started well before I could walk, feed myself, or had any significant use of my hands. My goal was to return to running again, hopefully even completing a marathon.

- **Breathe.** "Breathe," a mentor of my trauma survivor group wrote in her journal. That was key for me many times. I could have tensed up in the emergency room. But I somehow knew that I really should relax. When I am moderately still, I am aware of each heartbeat, so I would try to time my breathing to my heartbeats: breathe in on three heartbeats, breathe out on four; breathe in on four, out on four; breathe in on five, and so on. And so I relaxed, just focusing on breathing. Sleeping was a challenge for the first few months; many chemical sleep aids essentially require that you doze off within a few minutes, but ususally this breathing exercise was the only way I could do that.

- **A loving caregiver** can speed your recovery. My wife was with me for most of each day that I was in the hospital. My mentor, the leader of our trauma group, indicated that this was one of the most important indicators for success in recovery. Sometimes we talked, sometimes I just dozed off, but she was almost always with me. For the first couple of weeks, especially the first week, when I couldn't sleep, the night dragged on second by second, and I relished meeting the senior trauma resident at about 5:15 or 5:30 a.m. I hadn't thought about loneliness during this period, but it must have been there. The end of the nightly loneliness was one of the brighter moments of each day.

- **Divine caregiving and prayer.** I don't think I had any days without prayer, especially in the early evening, where it sometimes stretched out to a couple of hours. Sometimes I would just succumb to sleep or doze off, which I suppose was a needed response of grace. Most days as my wife was leaving, we would join in prayers of thanksgiving and petition, some about my healing.

I feel strongly that I have had divine assistance at least a couple of times in my psychological and physical healing, which has led to spiritual growth.

My mentor said, "You're going to cry a lot; you're going to have emotional issues." She also wrote, "It feels to me that as a young teenager... I said many times that I didn't have any emotions. When I was slightly older, I realized, yes, I did have anger. But I almost never cried. Now I cry a lot. Sometimes I cry from my own pain and frustration, somewhat more often from the pain and frustration of those around me. But far more often than either of those, I cry tears of joy about those who are doing what they can to help other people." In short, my mentor was overjoyed for those doing what Christ would do or what he would have us do.

My newfound ability to express emotions seems related to my metamorphosis from introversion to extroversion. I am a technical professional, an engineer; it is a stereotype that engineers have limited communication skills and that they aren't as good as others when it comes to soft "people skills." A friend joked with me that an extroverted engineer is one who looks at his shoes when he talks with you. Previously I had almost never felt comfortable being in a group of people new to me. Now I relish the opportunity for meeting new people and learning from them.

Each of my GWUH (George Washington University Hospital) trauma survivor group members individually believes that we are fortunate. This goes well beyond any similarities of trauma. A friend who has multiple sclerosis (MS) confided to me that having an incurable and fatal degenerative disease changed his perspective. It struck a chord with me when this world-class economist and statistician said, "About 10% of MS patients go into a tailspin, and about 30% don't come to a positive outlook, but 60% view themselves as being blessed and more focused."

I have frustrations, a lack of acceptance for what I can no longer do as easily or efficiently as I did before the accident. I made more errors when typing with my left hand; I dropped things more frequently with my left hand than with my right, but this is no longer an issue. More commonly now, the frustration is in dropping something that I don't think I would have had an issue hanging onto. Not a big deal. I'm just not as integrated or accepting of what I am. My friend with MS also indicated that he, too, is challenged with accepting what he can no longer do as easily—or at all.

Getting off painkillers was certainly an early goal. One morphine derivative had zero effect on my pain, but it took a few days for me to express that and for a change to be made; other painkillers were more effective. My biggest rationale for painkillers was being able to sleep, which was impossible without them. So I would take them in the evening, taking fewer during the day. For me, high pain levels were linked with very high blood pressure, so there was a risk in reducing the use of painkillers.

Even without the blood pressure monitor, I could usually tell when my blood pressure was going up in association with the pain, so sometimes I took the painkillers for that. I wasn't sure that I would be able to get myself off painkillers within a few weeks of going home, but because I rationed my painkillers, I was able to do that. The morning after coming home from the hospital, I felt my pain had increased, so I took my blood pressure pill, and my blood pressure dropped to 55/45. That was the last blood pressure medicine I took.

One year post-trauma, one of the questions that I discussed with my group was, "How was I doing at the end of eight months, and have I continued to steadily improve since then, contrary to the doctor's predictions?" The unanimous affirmation from the other members of the group was that eight months had not been the end of recovery for them. Neither had it been the maximum level of recovery for me. I am mostly better than I was at eight months. I can now do things that I could not do at eight months: I can do pushups and chin-ups, and I can run faster, though not as fast as I used to.

On the downside, I have lost some of the range of motion and strength in my injured shoulder since about five months post-trauma, when I was still receiving therapy. The obvious thing is to try to continue therapy just for that, but on a more focused basis. However, it has been a struggle with my insurance coverage. I have been trying unsuccessfully to resolve this issue for the past four months or so.

Though my fall was clearly my own fault, I haven't been down on myself. There is no point in that. But I do have frustrations about what I can't do or can't do as well. "Come on!!" seems almost like a daily or maybe hourly self-curse to me, though I think I've gotten better about that one over the last month.

With fairly intensive self-therapy (30 minutes twice a day, morning and evening) I can hold off further deterioration, but I'm not at all sure I am getting any better. Worse, I don't know if some of my self-therapy is making injury issues worse, rather than better. This too has been the experience of my colleagues, who have needed to return for therapy a few months after they thought they were finished. As one friend put it, he'd envisioned being able to "coast," once he got back to an acceptable level of recovery. Instead, self-therapy is a struggle every day. The downside of continuing the struggle is quite possibly arthritis, which could remove the ability to do that activity. Our orthopedic surgeon advised us separately that that is a likely outcome. I continue to have pain, sporadically, all days.

It was a struggle going back to work just four weeks after getting out of the hospital. I started with a couple of weeks working half-time. Initially I was tired, still in varying amounts of pain, and found it difficult to focus. Probably for about six months, my work was substandard in the fairly intense environment with many deadlines. Now I am in a position where I can mentor new hires, which I thoroughly enjoy. Time pressure or the inability to complete all of the projects continues, but perhaps a better grasp of communication and prioritization will help.

I am so glad for what I can learn from my peers in my trauma survivors' group and for what I can share with them. I've struggled through continuing most of the activities that I had a year ago, but the sharing with this group has been my most satisfying activity. I'm starting to visit patients new to surviving trauma, and hope to continue that in the hospital and other caregiving environments. I am more integrated, more accepting of myself than I was before the injury. I give thanks and praise for my remarkable surgeon, my medical team, my family, my newfound friends, and especially for my Savior and the faith that has pulled me through.

A month ago Paul bravely and confidently completed a competitive marathon. His family and job are back on track. His eldest daughter is about to graduate from law school. He is back on track with his engineering job, managing drinking water in Maryland. He has many new friends and good, deep, loving relationships. Paul has recovered from his traumatic accident to be even more joyful, successful, and at peace.

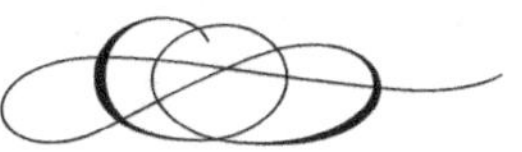

Chapter 8
Seek the Light in the Darkness

The abysmal darkness of alcoholism, drug addiction, domestic violence, divorce, depression, disease, and other tragedies affects untold numbers of families, but much of the darkness is hidden because of fear, pride, humiliation, or embarrassment and the lack of community and spiritual support. Darkness, deep darkness can potentially lead to tragedy. The following are the true stories of two good friends who have opened their hearts to share their stories and their healing. One friend suffered from emotional issues, alcoholism, and a life-threatening accident. The other faced a life-threatening disease and broken relationship with a loved one. They both miraculously survived, sought the light in the darkness, and refused to let go of their hope for the future. Today they are people filled with joy and very happy. These stories are based on my in-person interviews. Names have been changed to protect privacy.

Benny Finds the Light
by Jeff Cline

My friend Benny suffered many setbacks in his early years. He had a serious, life-threatening accident when he was only 20 years old. "I woke up in a hospital bed, asking, 'Where am I? How did I get here?' and moaning, 'Oh how I hurt.' "

His doctor replied, "You are very lucky to be alive, young man. You're in the hospital. You were brought here after an extremely bad accident involving your motorcycle and a truck." Benny's nearly fatal accident altered his life suddenly and dramatically.

During most of his early life, Benny suffered from depression, at times so overwhelming that he considered suicide. He was in darkness, unable to see the light. He was quite shy, and unable to develop strong relationships; he was effectively alone. Growing up poor in a remote home in the rural south did not help.

Without a purpose in life, Benny nonetheless attended college; however, he dropped out after three semesters with a 1.8 GPA. He partied hard and often, drinking and smoking excessively. Now he was in the hospital, in traction as a result of his considerable injuries. During his 63 days in the hospital and two more months handicapped by a body cast, Benny had plenty of time to think. He decided to go back to college. He enrolled at a nearby university, choosing to study business administration. His A's in accounting helped direct him to his ultimate career path. However, getting a college degree did nothing to create peace and happiness in his life, nor did it take away his depression.

Over coffee, Benny reminisced with me about his life after college graduation. As a graduate, he was hired out of college by a premier international accounting company. But even after getting the dream job, he did not find peace and happiness. When he met Charlene, whom he married six months later, his life appeared to be much improved. But something important was still missing; he hadn't found what he was looking for, so he remained depressed. He smoked and drank excessively and went out to nightclubs too often. After his daughter was born, his growing family increased Benny's responsibilities and deepened the feeling that something was seriously missing in his life. In April of 1975, while attending an evangelistic crusade, Benny said a prayer to accept the Lord into his life.

Therefore, since we have been justified through faith, we have peace with God through our Lord Jesus Christ, through whom we have gained access by faith into this grace in which we now stand. And we boast in the hope of the glory of God…we glory in our sufferings, because we know that suffering produces perseverance; perseverance, character; and character, hope. And hope does not put us to shame, because God's love has been poured out into our hearts through the Holy Spirit.

Romans 5:1-5

Benny had finally found the peace, hope, and happiness he had been searching for all of his life. His son was born six months later. His marriage with Charlene became a struggle during this time until she accepted the Lord back into her life. The family was coming together, now with love.

At this time, Benny decided to part with the large company he worked for and start his own firm. He quit drinking excessively and stopped smoking "cold turkey." With improving self-confidence, Benny's firm quickly became profitable.

Benny and Charlene joined a church, where he took on a leadership role. He began teaching bible lessons to adults and children. He altered his personal and business lives to accord with Christian principles; the most obvious act was quitting smoking and stopping excessive drinking. Benny was no longer depressed. His self-image greatly improved as he loved the Lord, his family, and himself. He began developing deep relationships, and his business was growing rapidly. He helped to form and lead growth groups at church, each becoming a basis for individuals to make deep friendships. Helping others grow in their love of the Lord and of each other was rewarding, giving him joy and satisfaction. Instead of being depressed, he was relaxed, happy, and at peace.

As the president of his firm, Benny would become acutely stressed and very anxious over issues with clients, particularly when very important financial problems arose as a result of his company's involvement. Benny insisted on always doing the right thing. In fact, when he discovered that his firm had made a substantial mistake of over a million dollars for a client company, he began taking anti-anxiety medication to control his stress level. He prayed for guidance to manage the situation. He worked with the client company to correct the mistake, convincing them to make late payments. The company management admired Benny's honesty and made the payments. In fact, they still remain a client of Benny's firm. Benny explained, "Major things can knock you down, but smaller things can break you down, especially if you do not face them and deal with them, always doing what is right."

"I quit the anti-anxiety medications "cold turkey" as soon as I retired," Benny told me. He philosophized, "My peace and contentment are justified by my faith. Peace ends depression. They are mutually exclusive. Peace comes by standing with the Lord, and this helps me and us to endure. Suffering produces endurance, endurance produces character, and character produces hope." Now Benny garners pride and much joy from his passion as a Master Gardener. He helps the local community nurture their own gardens and micro-environments, and with enthusiasm, he teaches the basics of gardening to primary education students.

Benny's life journey began with the deep darkness of serious, almost overwhelming depression, resulting in no friends, no purpose, no hope or joy. His attitude and behavior took him deeper into a dark place. Then a prayer to the Lord at a revival changed his life. He accepted the Lord, finally finding what he had been seeking his entire life.

Benny has had serious lows since, especially with his company, but not the deep darkness. He has dealt with the issues directly with a Christian conscience and applied principles. He learned from his lows, especially his deep, dark lows. With fortitude and hope, he just got up and moved in a positive direction, ultimately finding success and joy with his family and business, while rejecting depression and victimhood. His adult children are successful and happy, bringing Benny and his wife lovable grandchildren. He and his wife of over 40 years now live comfortably in a condition of peace, contentment and joy.

Jack's Wisdom Leads to Joy
by Jeff Cline

Jack is an especially joyful, contented friend, the kind of positive, buoyant guy you like to hang around with. One day, when we were having coffee together in a hotel cafeteria, I asked Jack what his secret was. "Well first, I always start my day with a prayer to be happy." He continued, "Second, happiness is a *conscious* decision I make often." Jack is the director of engineering for a large hotel. The stress of satisfying the demands of owners and management, as well as hotel customers, can be pressing, leading to anxiety, anger, and frustration. "I become anxious sometimes, but never angry," Jack said. "Anger, anxiety, boredom—these are choices and I choose not to suffer them."

Jack practices integrity, reason, and logic in all aspects of his life, both at home and at work, where he is highly respected by management as well as those who report to him. He is open, forthright, honest, and loyal with his management and with his co-workers as well. Jack believes his important role in life is to encourage others, which he does abundantly. He expects others around him to do as he does: work hard and effectively at the assigned duties and goals. He likes to see that his people really enjoy their work and are enthusiastic team members who contribute to the success of the hotel. Jack said, "Through hard work, a positive attitude, serving the needs of the hotel and customers, the money will come."

Jack told me that his life began after he graduated from college as an electrical engineer. He joined the Navy, where he quickly advanced to lieutenant commander, assuming a major leadership role managing several departments on ships transporting Marines and combat equipment during the Vietnam War era. He made a point to respect the enlisted men, which he explained was a trait of a true leader. "You must make people believe in you," he said. "Then you can help them believe in themselves, another aspect of a true leader." By applying this philosophy, Jack was able to inspire his enlisted men to achieve the seemingly impossible, especially under fire. He described his ship's captain as a good man, with mutual respect between them. The captain wrote a glowing letter of commendation for Jack. He said, "Jack has the best ship handling skills of any person I have ever met." However, Jack's potential navy career ended after ten years because his family was a higher priority.

Jack was widowed when his first wife died of cancer. He has now been married to Lilly for eight years. "I have never had an argument with either wife, during a total of 31 years of marriage," he said. "When we are angry and argue, hurtful things are said that cannot be taken back." Jack has always chosen to let himself and his wife cool down, and only then discuss the issue frankly and resolve it. He has had a deep and loving relationship with both wives.

Jack has five adult children: a biological son, two adopted sons, and a daughter whom Lilly brought to the marriage. With a joyful smile, he spoke of his special feelings of love when holding the children as babies. He said, "This demonstrates the power of love from God, which helps us to love babies, even if they are not our own biological children." He raised all five children, loving them unconditionally. "At times," he said, "I was disappointed in their behavior, but I still loved them. I practiced "tough love," because a good parent must not enable bad behavior. Furthermore, a good parent should not make or allow their child to become dependent. Instead, the parent should help their children become independent and responsible for their behavior. We parents must do our job to set our children up to be successful. I believe that too many parents actually handicap their children. Because of this irresponsible parenting, we now have the 'me' generation, people who are entirely self-centered, expecting everything to be handed to them. They lack responsibility and good moral character and are unable to develop deep relationships. They think the world revolves around them. As a result, today's youth in America are highly anxious, unhappy, and without hope for the future. But my children, in contrast, are really good, happy, successful people."

Should you think that Jack is so filled with joy because he has never had any problems, think again. He has had many serious life crises. His parents divorced when he was five, and he never saw his biological father again. He lost his close 16-year-old brother in a motorcycle accident. Then he lost his wife to cancer after 23 years of marriage. Jack's second wife, Lilly, is recovering from an epic battle with lymphoma, a blood cancer. Speaking of his relationship with his wives, Jack said, "I seek to go through life hand and hand with my spouse, not one dragging the other down. Most of us are coming into a crisis, are in a crisis, or coming out of a crisis. Life moves on, and each of us must move on as well. We must never give up, but just get up after a crisis and continue life in a positive direction."

I asked Jack how to best manage recovery from a crisis. "An optimist sees a glass as half full, and a pessimist sees a glass as half empty. However, I like to think of the glass as twice as high as it needs to be, especially after a crisis. I will not play the losers game of 'why me' or 'why now'! Crises—deep dark times—happen to all of us, everyone around the world. This is all according to God's plan, and there is nothing we can do about it. It just happens when it does. Everyone in these difficult life circumstances, including myself, has a responsibility to respond positively, while learning from the crises. We must forgive and not stumble over something already behind us. We must see the crisis as a learning experience."

"What activity brings you joy?" I asked. Jack gave a specific example. "I have a gift of woodworking, looking at things, and being able to fix them. I focus fully on applying these abilities. I become a different person when I am building things— happy, contented, relaxed. I also become a different, more relaxed person when captaining a boat on the water. My anxiety simply melts away. I also pray to God to help me deal with the grief of a crisis. For me, I can become happy, even after a crisis, by letting go of what is gone, being grateful for my remaining blessings, burying myself in my passions, and looking forward to the good opportunities coming."

This man I admire so much is dedicated to helping others. He mentors young men at the Tulsa Boys Home. Most of these young men come from toxic environments: single-parent homes rampant with drug use, or homes with physical and emotional abuse or mental illness. Some of the boys have been in multiple foster homes. Jack works with these boys from a basis of strong Christian principles, love and care, demonstrating to the boys what a normal life can be like. The goal is for many to leave the Tulsa Boys Home to become productive, positive members of society with a life based on Christian principles

Jack has also worked with people in hospice care, where he has found it an honor to become someone's friend before they die. In that role, Jack has observed that once people give up, they die quickly. He believes we are supposed to help others through life, which helps one to be filled with joy and be happy in their own life. "After a crisis, I recover more quickly through helping others, because it gives me immense joy," he said. "My secret to being happy is giving to others by passing on wisdom, donating to charity, funding good causes, and helping the elderly. Life is not easy or effortless, but it is worth living if you choose a positive path of hope and loving and helping others."

In summary, Jack is happy and contented with a loving, successful family. He manages his life with the principles he advocates for all: take the focus off yourself by reaching out to help others.

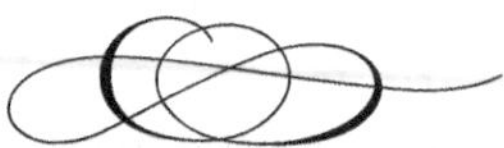

Chapter 9

Finding Peace, Contentment, and Joy

People are just about as happy as they make up their minds to be.
Abraham Lincoln

Happiness is a fundamental natural pursuit in which a person devotes themselves to the things in life that bring them the most pleasure and joy, as is illustrated in the stories of heroes and heroines in this chapter.

David's Story
by Jeff Cline
(Name changed out of respect for privacy)

As he and I were reflecting about our lives, David, with his typical smile and a little chuckle, shared his philosophy of life. He had recently retired from a thirty-year career in the oil industry during which he had survived twenty-five layoffs. This would fill many people with acute anxiety, anger, and discouragement. However, David not only survived, but was happy and contented with his life. David's secret to survival was keeping a positive attitude and doing his job, going out of his way to serve his manager and his team. He said, "I personally believe that accepting Jesus Christ is the key to happiness and joy. Plus, I have a small group of reliable friends who have my back. I have a spouse who loves me. Joy is a choice; it is contentment."

David emphasized, "Forgiveness is an important part of being happy." In his career, family life, and with friends and associates, David tries hard to understand and not be judgmental of others who may be treating him poorly or unfairly. While he stands up for himself and his family, he refuses to worry, seek revenge, or become angry, but rather forgives and moves on. He added, "I also regularly enjoy quiet times, walking in the woods and seeing God's wonderful creation, reflecting on his blessings, and my good fortune. I have hope in the future, because I have a redeemer, Jesus Christ."

But David wonders if young Americans who are moving away from the church are losing hope. "Our young people today are typically self-centered. They don't realize their blessings. And they aren't interested in participating positively in our society." In his experience as a guide on mission trips to Mexico and Guatemala, he believes third world kids are happier than their American counterparts. "If American youth would help others, they would become less self-centered, less stressed, and they'd be happier. They need to focus on loving their neighbor as themselves," he added.

"Helping others less fortunate has given me much happiness," reflected David. He believes the real champions in life are those who help others without applause or recognition. "To help others less fortunate," David said, "you must first treat people with dignity and respect. Then they will accept your help. You must listen if you are to truly understand how you can help them best."

Currently David uses his skills to help others. He builds cabinets for Habitat for Humanity's houses being built for poor families. He's on the board of Youth at Heart, which helps children of disadvantaged families to enjoy the opportunities that America has to offer. With a smile, he explained, "Helping poor people with few resources is very rewarding to me, bringing me joy and happiness. My faith has changed my life in many positive ways and made seemingly unattainable goals like contentment and happiness, readily attainable. I'm content with my life, I'm filled with joy, and I have hope in the future."

> *I am not saying this because I am in need, for I have learned to be content whatever the circumstances.*
> Paul, Philippians 4:11

Charlie's Story, the Wisdom of an Elder
by Jeff Cline
(Name changed out of respect for privacy)

My dear friend Charlie is always a pleasure to be with. He is always happy, greeting me and others with a welcoming, loving, and kind smile.

One day, he proudly introduced me to his new wife, Gay. Gay is beautiful inside and out. Later, when I was probing Charlie a little about any crises in his life, he reluctantly admitted to a period of depression. "I lost my first wife, whom I loved with all my heart, after over 50 years of a wonderful marriage. For a year I buried myself in my business. Then I realized I was terribly depressed. At every opportunity I began talking to friends about my loss. After two years, I finally was ready to just get up and move on. With the Lord's help and guidance, I met Gay, who had recently lost her husband. We fell in love, and remarried, resulting in each of us emerging from our depression and restoring the joy we had lost. The Lord has always guided me to think positively and not accept the negative. As a salesman, I had a lifetime of disappointments. So what? I just moved on, optimistic that a sales success was coming."

Charlie engages people quickly, becoming a sincere friend who is honest, frank, uncomplicated, and always optimistic. He is a man of few words, yet most listen closely for his wisdom when offered because he is so wise. In fact, Charlie offered me a valuable nugget of wisdom one day when he said, "The most difficult thing to achieve is to listen. You must learn to listen better and allow others to communicate with you. In so doing, a person often discovers himself."

Charlie's foremost purpose in life today is to help others. He enjoys supporting nursing homes, where he offers kindly encouragement and laughter to the "younger" residents. Incidentally, Charlie is 87, older than most in the nursing homes. He is a blessing to the young and old. At his church, he teaches Sunday school to preschoolers. He listens and offers wisdom to the teens at the Tulsa Boys Home. He mused, "My secret to being happy comes from giving to others by passing on wisdom, donating time to charity, funding good causes, helping the elderly, and educating children." He believes we all have a responsibility to laugh, be joyful, smile, and encourage others, as he does.

Charlie's simple advice for joy in life: Let the past go, pray about everything, accept what life gives you, forgive others who have hurt you and forgive yourself, focus on what's good in life, help others, and enjoy this moment." As an afterthought he added, "Look upon curses as blessings."

Two Women of Noble Character
by Jeff Cline

In Proverbs 31: 10-31, King Lemuel describes the virtues of strong and noble women. These are stories of two women who are shining examples of strength and nobility, who found peace and contentment by having a positive attitude, optimism, and focusing on the light.

MJ Glows with Optimism

This is the story of my cousin MJ, of whom I am in awe. She has chosen to just stand up after each crisis and optimistically move on, refusing to dwell in victimhood or anger. Rather, she has accepted responsibility for her decisions and her life, always choosing a positive path forward.

Recently, Nancy and I enjoyed dinner with MJ and her husband of 19 years at their beautiful home in a wooded area of southern Wisconsin. When I told her I was writing a book, she shared the story of her challenging early life, which was filled with crises. At seven, she suffered life-changing trauma from the divorce of her parents. Suddenly, she, her four siblings, and her unemployed mother were left to survive without the support of a father and husband. Her mother was a basket case. She could not drive. She had simply been a mother who took care of the household after marrying a World War II Veteran and policeman.

"I was ashamed. I felt guilty. I believed I was the cause of the divorce," MJ said. She lost many relationships. She was shunned by so-called friends. She and her siblings lost contact with the relatives on her father's side. They were often unable to attend gatherings on my side of the family because they did not have the financial means to do so. In the beginning, everyone in the family took buses everywhere. New clothes were now hand-me-downs, some of which came from my mother, MJ's aunt. Yet MJ described herself with a chuckle. "I have always been an optimist, seeing my cup as half full rather than half empty. I always had hope for a better life. And, I was stubborn; I would never give up. I just got up and moved on."

MJ decided to go to a two-year college at first and then go on to obtain a medical degree. She hadn't any financial support, so she worked part-time and attended classes part-time. When she graduated from the two-year medical program, an advisor recommended that she seek a four-year degree as planned. MJ enjoyed helping people and saw the four-year medical degree as the next step in fulfilling her destiny. However, she became pregnant by her long-time boyfriend. They did not marry, so MJ became a single parent with the birth of her only daughter. More college was not feasible at this time in her life

Nevertheless, MJ continued to have hope. "Hope is everything," she said. "Living without hope is the worst thing. With hope, there is always the possibility of a better tomorrow."

"Did you seek social services help like welfare?" I asked. She exclaimed, "Absolutely not! That would be giving up. I was stubborn, and confident that I could make it on my own. It was against my moral principles to ask others, even the taxpayer, to bail me out of the situation for which I was responsible." MJ's moral character and strength were a marvel to me. Indeed, her decision not to marry her long-time boyfriend just because she was pregnant ultimately allowed her the opportunity to meet and marry the love of her life.

Her father passed away in 1991. The loss deeply saddened her and her siblings because they had attained a better relationship with him. They and their mother had all forgiven him for the divorce. MJ was devastated and felt like an orphan. About that time, Alzheimer's began to seriously affect her mother. MJ softly moaned, "I lost my mother twice, first to Alzheimer's and then when she died as a result in 1999."

"Didn't you also have a battle with breast cancer in about 2003? How did you make it?" I asked. She became thoughtful, and then replied, "First of all, I did not blame God. My belief in the Lord was essential to survival and recovery. With prayer came comfort and hope and relief from anxiety. Plus, during the time I had breast cancer, my husband, Bob, was a loving, supportive caregiver. God encourages us to have supportive family and to participate in communities of faith; he encourages us to be there to support one another during difficult times. We need to help one another, which makes us all feel better. It is better to give than to receive, don't you think?"

"Bob and I met by accident in 1999. He was divorced, with five children at home. We fell in love and married, giving me a companion and a family all at once. Now we have moved into our dream home, where all of our children and my siblings gather in love and companionship. I work two jobs, both of them in the medical field, where I help people with health problems. Bob is successful in his real estate business. We may not be able to retire until we are 70, but so what? My life journey has dealt me some severe setbacks. I never gave up, but just got up, always with determination to move forward with hope and optimism. I have left past crises behind me without regret. I love my children, husband, siblings, and our many friends. Isn't that what is most important, what makes life worth living? We are incredibly happy." Bob interjected, "MJ is perfect in every way." "Yes, that she is," I replied with a smile.

Alice Finds Joy

"I'm not leaving, even though they said I must. I'm not leaving here till the Lord gives me peace, and I know that's not happening, so I'm here for the duration. Squatters rights!" Alice sobbed mournfully as she lay in bed with only a jug of water, now for the third day. She refused to leave her room until she had peace, and she had absolutely no expectation of peace. She prayed to Jesus for counsel. "Give me strength, give me hope to stay in my home, which is not an option, or die." On the third day the Lord's peace flooded over her, and she responded, "Lord, what do you want me to do? What shall I do?"

Alice and Rob had met three days before with a marriage counselor, who they hoped would help them heal their crumbling relationship after a marriage of nineteen years. During the session, Rob was given an ultimatum to choose between Alice and their fourteen-year-old son. He chose their son. Alice was horrified. She drove home and crawled into bed with the jug of water, deeply depressed. She said gloomily, "I was in my deepest, darkest low." During the third day in bed, the Lord prompted Alice, after giving her his peace, "Get out of bed and seek help from your best-buddy girlfriends!"

Alice and her five girlfriends met that day for an emergency lunch. She was blunt. "Rob has chosen to live with Benjamin over me. I've been told we have to separate, and I must move out." Alice emotionally described the counseling session in which Rob had chosen their son over her. She was not thinking divorce, just healing through structured separation.

Alice, in the Lord's perfect peace, but still in shock, told her friends of her plight. "As you all know, I have no job. I have been on disability for seven years, ever since the automobile accident left me disabled and in and out of a wheelchair. Now it seems I may not have a home, a husband, nor possibly, even children." She became tearful. Immediately, her five friends formed a team to help, relegating responsibilities among themselves. One offered Alice a temporary place to stay. The group, whom Alice kindly referred to as TRAMPS after the first letters of their names, established a prayer partner group, complete with accountability to answer to important life questions.

"On that day with my five best buddies, I began to write five gratitudes every day, which helped save my life." Alice went on to talk about her feelings. "At times I would get angry and descend into victimhood. But God gave me hope for a better future. I was seeing what the Lord was doing in my life and I gave him glory through it all. He was walking me through, often carrying me through. I would get angry, but sadness was the bigger problem. Anger is a decision. I would choose to pray. The anger would stop when I prayed. Somewhere between the ages of three and five my daughter learned to say, when I was recovering from rageaholism, "Mom, let's pray," because that was my line to her when I caught myself yelling at her." Alice's relationship with Rob was sliding down a slippery slope, one that was leading beyond a structured separation.

Alice adjusted her morning routine to give the Lord the glory by beginning every day reading the Bible and seeking God's grace. Then at night she ended every day by thanking him for what he had done that day by listing five gratitudes; early on they were simply things like sunrises and sunsets, air to breathe, life, good friends. Alice admitted that initially, in extreme grief, it was difficult to find a single gratitude.

Alice's childhood experiences had set the stage for this family tragedy. On the good side, when she was seven years old, her grandmother took her to church, where she accepted Jesus as her Savior. There she learned her lifelong theme song, "Jesus Loves Me." During her teenage years her mother was suicidal. She described her father as a narcissist, a rageaholic (a person prone to extreme anger with little or no provocation). Alice admits, "I was a rageaholic just like my father when I began to raise my family. In my late teens my parents divorced. I was devastated and vowed that I would never, ever get divorced if I got married."

Alice attended Vanderbilt University, majoring in nursing. Describing herself, she said, "I was outgoing and an optimist. I kept Jesus very close." She became engaged to Rob just before graduation. Rob was nine years older and a successful businessman. They married and lived in Denver where she grew up.

After three years of marriage, Rob got a new job in Oklahoma. Alice stayed behind to have a baby daughter and sell the house. Then, while unpacking her belongings after the move to Oklahoma, Alice ruptured three disks in her back and was hospitalized. She ended up alone in Denver for six long months while she recovered. "I was fortunate that I didn't become a paraplegic," she said. "I recovered with daily prayer, physical therapy, and without surgery. But my relationship with Rob had become strained with our long separation. As a result, he asked me for a divorce when our baby daughter and I arrived in Oklahoma." This was a serious blow to Alice, but she would not give up. She convinced Rob to try communication sessions with just the Holy Spirit, with no family counseling together. After several months the relationship was repaired. A baby son was born three years later.

Then tragedy struck Alice when she was in a near-fatal automobile accident. She was never hospitalized because she was in shock and had post concussion syndrome. The day after the accident the doctor placed her on bed rest for six months. Alice was 100% disabled and often confined to a wheelchair. It was five years before she was able to drive again. People at her Baptist Church family helped her. Alice declared emphatically, "My relationship with Jesus gave me hope.

Numerous family counselors were hired by Alice and fired by Rob before 2001. It was in the final session that the counselor asked Rob to choose whom he would most like to live with. When Rob chose his son, it was the beginning of the end. A structured separation began, or so Alice thought. Rob thought otherwise, stating emphatically, "Our relationship and marriage are broken beyond repair. I have filed for divorce."

Alice lamented, "We had two teenagers who were hurt by our separation and even more hurt by our divorce. I plummeted into a deep depression, hitting rock-bottom as the tragedy of divorce unfolded." Alice sobbed, "Jesus Christ saved my life then."

Alice still lists her gratitudes each day. Her gratitudes are about giving God the glory by thanking him for what he has done, creating a positive ending to the day. To survive through the tragedy of her broken relationship, Alice said, "You must look at the good, God's good in life. A strong relationship with Jesus Christ my Lord is most essential. My road to recovery began when God showered me with his peace." She continued, "Also, support from my close friends (the TRAMPS) and the Celebrate Recovery group sessions were quite important in my healing."

Celebrate Recovery is a twelve-step program, which Joy Alice completed religiously. She received a sponsor and became a sponsor. Then she began to lead a Celebrate Recovery small group in a study featuring Rick Warren's *The Purpose Driven Life*. This helped her to get outside of herself, outside of her own problems." Today she remains engaged in Celebrate Recovery, the organization that helped her to restore her life. The physical healing took twelve years. The emotional and spiritual healing took even longer. In summary, the following strategies were used by Alice.

- She gave herself to her best friends at an initial meeting. God's wisdom flowed through them to her.

- She established a nightly routine of writing her gratitudes, her blessings, for the day.

- She recited daily the mnemonics RECEIVE (Reach, Enthusiastically, Christ, Expecting, Internal, Victory Everlasting) and TRUST (Total, Relax, Under, Savior, Transformation).

- She prayed daily and established accountability for her actions.

- She writes scripture verses on 3 x 5 cards daily to achieve peace and joy.

- She became active in the Celebrate Recovery group.

Recovery was slow but purposeful for Alice. She did not trust men and did not develop any relationships. Then she met John, who was also volunteering at Good Samaritan. They became friends, interacting only in group settings initially. Alice was finally building a relationship with a man, building relationships by living through the "Fruit of the Spirit." *But the fruit of the Spirit is love, joy, peace, patience, kindness, goodness, faithfulness, gentleness and self-control.* Galatians 5:22-23

Today Alice is dedicated to helping others. As a nurse at Good Samaritan she daily helps provide medical attention to those without medical access through insurance. She travels on mission trips to bring the opportunity of Lord Jesus to many, even in the Middle East. She has been the director of a Christian prison ministry, helping to rehabilitate incarcerated women through the love of God, teaching them to love their neighbor as themselves.

Speaking with great emotion, Alice said, "With the physical and emotional challenges in dark times, especially those that are life threatening, you must keep your eyes on Jesus, look full in his wonderful face and never give up, but maintain hope in him. This is reflected in one of my life verses, Acts 17:28, *In Him we live, move and have our being.* "In my modified life after a difficult, dark time, filled with the joy of the Lord, I took up my cross and followed him. I walk now in his peace, joy, love and the other fruits of the Spirit, which give me hope and a positive attitude. A person can recover from severe crises through the power of the Holy Spirit and joy from the Lord. When finally at peace and filled with hope, one can choose to be happy, successful, and of help to others. The life-giving love of God, friends, and family is essential. It is a choice to find the joy of the Lord through painful things and remembering suffering. Happiness does not come without enduring some unhappy times. Grief, sorrow and melancholy are a choice, just as is happiness. My faith has changed my life in many positive ways and made seemingly unattainable goals like joy and happiness readily attainable."

Alice acquired a nickname and is now called Joy Alice by friends. She often hums her theme song, "Jesus Loves Me." She builds strong relationships with many, both men and women. Joy Alice will continue this path until the end. She thinks the following epitaph will be appropriate:

<h2 style="text-align:center">End of construction
Thank you for your patience.</h2>

Chapter 10

Financial and Business Distress

Crises do not always come primarily in the form of broken relationships, illnesses, or the death of a loved one. Sometimes the major crisis is financial or business-related and accompanied by the heartbreak of letting people down in spite of your best efforts. The stories of these friends illustrate Ernest Hemingway's definition of courage: "Courage is grace under pressure."

From the Heights to the Depths and Back
by a follower of Jesus

Have you ever felt you were in the center of God's will? I have. After much hard work and sacrifice, I had climbed the corporate ladder to the top of a large, fully-integrated energy company. My loving wife of 40 years had been most supportive. She had dedicated herself to teaching others the Word of God and raising our two children, then in college. Their faith in Jesus was rock solid, and they were prepared to fly the nest. As a family we were a strong and interdependent unit. My wife and I were very involved in our church, participating in several small groups and mission-type projects. We were investing financially in the Lord's work through a number of other organizations as well. Everything was in order.

Unexpectedly, a competing company made an offer for my company that we could not refuse. So in a matter of a few months, the thing in which I had invested 20 years of my time, energy, and thoughts was gone. That company had been my baby, my life. It had provided a platform for me to grow and prosper, to use my talents to bless others, internally and externally. It was a wonderful place to work. Though the company was large, we worked hard to make it feel like a small team, a family. We were successful, and we did it while holding on to key principles, such as integrity, responsibility, relationships and accountability. Now it all vanished in a flash.

But all was not lost. Due to my position within the company I was afforded a very large severance package—a golden parachute. We were able to make substantial gifts to our favorite charities. I invested the remaining money in the acquiring company. Financially secure at such an early age, I believed I would never need to work for a paycheck again. Shortly thereafter, I agreed to join the board of directors of a German-owned energy company. That allowed me to keep my head in the business world and in the energy game.

Then another exciting opportunity was presented. I was asked to go on staff at my church. My wife and I had been members of this 7,500 member congregation since our college years. This seemed like a perfect way to utilize my talents and give back to a very special place. I loved it. I was able to incorporate business aspects, such as goals, objectives, and strategies, into the church environment. We crystallized our mission: *To honor God and make Disciples of Christ.* We built a new church and relocated it to a new, state-of-the-art campus. We bought a communist youth camp in Estonia and turned it into a youth camp for Jesus. We started significant other mission initiatives in places like Tanzania, Mexico, and Guatemala. We were on a roll.

But a major problem then developed. My investment in the acquiring company began to sink...and fast. Much like Enron before, it had entered into terrible positions that took it down financially. The stock value cratered from $53 to $0.79 cents per share. I could not get out fast enough. In the middle of the free fall I was called to Germany for a meeting. Halfway around the world, I was cut off from all my support: my wife, the men in my small groups, and my advisors. I was isolated, I believe by God's plan, not life circumstances.

I thought I was in God's perfect will. What went wrong? That night in a German hotel room I had a fight with God. Not just an ordinary questioning of *why God, why me?* But a knock down, yelling, screaming match, pillow and mattress throwing, crying, hair pulling, night-long fight. He had me cornered. He had my undivided attention. He had me where he wanted me—isolated. And he had me exactly where I needed to be. Stripped bare. One-on-one with the one true living God.

No sleep that night—not a moment. I left that hotel room the next morning broke and broken. But somewhat surprisingly, I felt some peace. My financial security was gone. In my heart I knew he loved me, he cared, he would provide.

I boarded the plane for the long flight home. I could not wait. I walked into the new home we just had finished building and fell into my wife's arms. I said, "I have lost it all." She said, "I know. It's okay. I love you." I was a wreck. She was solid. She never wavered.

I knew the game was over. I was humbled. God had stripped me of all my pride. I had to find a paying job. I had to leave my church position. I had been out of the workforce for five years. Where to start? My contacts, my industry knowledge—all were stale. I had little to offer. My trust had to be in the Lord. I found it was one thing to accept Jesus and his promise of eternal life and a different thing to be totally dependent on him on a daily basis. Suffering is a part of living. Jesus suffered in life and in death. Why should I expect anything more? It is how you respond that reveals your true character.

During my rather short tenure at the church I had been advising a young man who had started his own real estate business. He knew the business. I did not. He did not know how to grow a business, but I did. In short, we formed a partnership, and for the next ten years I was the president of a company in an industry I knew nothing about. Isn't that just like God? Well, we grew it by a factor of ten. We created a culture based on core values around—you guessed it—integrity, responsibility, relationships, and accountability. We hand-selected every individual hired, filtering applicants by those core values. We took lawyers, accountants, MBAs, salesmen, tech execs and transformed them into real estate gurus. It was fun. It was rewarding. After a ten-year run I decided to step down, though I remain on the board of advisors.

I am a cancer survivor. My wife is a two-time cancer survivor. We are survivors of a financial crisis. Now I am 70 years old and married to the same loving wife. Our five grandchildren know Jesus as their Lord and Savior. We are financially restored and retired once again. But, I am convinced God is not done with us yet.

I am overwhelmed by God's love, protection, and provision. We have learned to praise him in the good times and the bad. When I came to him with my heart in pieces, I found he had healing. He makes all things new. He is the true source of all wisdom. I place my trust in him for today and eternity.

There is a contemporary Christian song, written by Matt and Beth Redman and recorded on their 2003 album "Where Angels Fear to Tread" that I find especially meaningful:

Blessed be Your Name
In the land that is plentiful
Where Your streams of abundance flow...

God you give and take away
Oh you give and take away
My heart will choose to say
Lord, blessed be Your name
Blessed be Your Name . . .

I pray my story will bless and help heal all those who suffer,

A follower of Jesus

Gary and Ann — Saved
by Jeff Cline

In this story, my friend Gary relates how God can alter a person's life path 180° if his commandments are followed. Gary, now a successful businessman, went from delinquent hippie to loving family man through a miracle. During their 44 years of marriage, Gary and his wife, Ann, have emerged from serious crises and challenging circumstances, to be joyful, contented, and hopeful.

At dinner one night, Nancy and I asked Gary and Ann how they had met and married. Gary began by describing who he was before he met Ann. "I was a long-haired hippie, undisciplined, very much into drugs, and sort of a rascal."

Gary began his story with an incident that happened in high school That morning he sat indignantly before the dean of boys, sent there yet again for discipline problems pertaining to his length of hair. The dean calmly explained, "Gary, if you come back on Monday, and your hair isn't above your collar, you will be suspended for three days. If you refuse to cut your hair, I will expel you from school."

Gary countered, "I'm not going to cut my hair, so I'll save you the trouble of expelling me. I'll quit school now, and I'm not coming back, ever!" Gary, who was a sophomore and just 15, assumed that because he was not yet 16 the dean would say, "No! You're not 16 yet."

To his great surprise, Gary discovered that it was not necessary to be 16 to quit. His bluff failed. The dean just said, "Okay, have it your way." The dean was apparently relieved to be finally rid of this character, with his poor grades, typically

D's, and F's, and his drug-dealing on campus. This kid was a troublemaker who was a bad influence on the other students. Even though he was shocked at first, his outlook changed to, "Yippee, now I'll have the freedom to do whatever I want to do."

Gary followed the bridge-burning at school with an expletive-laced argument with his father. "I'm moving out. I don't like you and the way you harass me, and I can do better on my own."

Gary went on. "I moved in with a hippie friend just like me. I got a job in grounds maintenance at a local golf course. I walked or hitchhiked everywhere. So, you can see, I was late to work and just as unreliable there as I had been at school. I was a chain smoker, I used profane language, and I smoked grass every day. We thought that life would be perfect now, if only we had more money."

One evening Gary and his friend Graham were contemplating breaking into the golf facilities to steal money that they had convinced themselves they deserved. Gary's older brother, Richard, happened to be staying with him temporarily because he was between apartments. One evening, when his brother was going out with older friends, Gary and Graham decided to go out and party elsewhere. The conversation turned to girls, so they decided to go down to "The Pit," a huge park where all the hippies gathered to buy and sell drugs. Once there, Graham started to complain that his girlfriend was not at the Pit, but had gone instead with a couple of girlfriends to a Rock Opera at the West Palm Beach Auditorium. He complained so much that Gary just gave up partying and said, "Okay, lets hitchhike to the event and find her." After arriving they followed the flow and found themselves at a concert called "Show Me Jesus." They decided to go in and see what it was all about.

Gary, always the salesman, talked the gatekeeper into letting them in for free. Meanwhile, Ann, who had recently been saved, had come separately with several invited girlfriends, one of whom happened to be Graham's girlfriend. They had taken their seats in the lower section close to the stage. Gary and his friends started out high up in the J section of the auditorium.

Ann and her friends knew who Gary and Graham were, but didn't know they were at the concert. Gary was emotionally overcome by the music. The storyline of the musical hit home, and he was drawn to the message of the show. The lead role in the play was a guy just like Gary, who was lost as well. But deep down he was asking serious questions about his life.

After the music ended, a pastor made an altar call. Gary, who had begun to sober up, approached the stage with his friends in tow. "I was drawn to the stage," Gary said. "We all marched up onto the stage together." Ann and her friends had been praying for Gary and his friends and saw them heading toward the stage. They saw them bow down and pray the sinner's prayer. The minister led a prayer, "Let Jesus into your life, be sorry for what you have done, repent, and you will be saved."

Gary exclaimed emotionally, "I was overcome with the Lord. A light was turned on. Suddenly my life changed to the positive. For the first time, I had a purpose in life, and I could see it. I had hope. I made a decision to follow the teachings of Jesus. I was no longer interested in partying or drugs. I suddenly wanted to have a loving relationship with the Lord and other people." Meanwhile, Ann and her friends joined Gary and Graham behind the stage after the concert ended.

Gary and his friends got a ride to their apartment, arriving at ten. This was unusual because most evenings ended after two in the morning. Gary's brother was already home. As Gary approached the door, his brother opened it. "What are you doing home so early?"

Gary exclaimed passionately, "I was saved tonight."

"You what?"

Gary, with somewhat less confidence repeated, "I got saved tonight..." Then, surprising them both, Richard proclaimed proudly, "I got saved tonight too!" They started to compare notes, and Richard explained that he had been at a hash party that night with friends; they'd been listening to the album *Tommy*, the rock opera by The Who. When God spoke to Richard through the lyrics and the images on the cover, he realized that he needed to return to the faith of his childhood and commit his life to Christ. The brothers had simultaneously been saved at the same moment, but in different places.

"Now the hard work began," Gary said. "I had to ask forgiveness from the many I had offended, especially my parents. They took me back, but with reservations in the beginning." A healthy, loving parent/child relationship began to grow. The pastor Fenton Moorehead, who had given the altar call at the concert that night, and the principal, Dr. Eissey, happened to be friends and had talked about Gary. Fenton assured him that Gary had truly become a Christian. The principal reluctantly accepted him back, once he was certain that his errant student had actually changed.

Gary now had a thirst for knowledge, and learning came easy for him now that he could concentrate. With his attitude change, he was cooperative with teachers. His goal was to graduate with his class, and once he set his mind to it, he began to get A's and B's.

At school, Ann and Gary's deep friendship eventually led to dating. Gary had begun to love someone besides himself. They married after graduation. Although they were only 18 and 19, they pledged a total commitment to each other and to spending their lives together living under the commandments of the Lord.

Ann's parents even agreed to the marriage, as long as Gary would agree that Ann would pursue a college degree. However, after a year of college, Ann became pregnant with their first child and this derailed the agreement. Nevertheless, her parents were happy because they had a grandbaby on the way. All this occurred just as Gary entered engineering school, where he spent two futile years pursuing a civil engineering degree. Fatherhood and financial needs started to crowd out his class schedule and study time. Keeping the family fed and a roof over their heads took priority over college. This led Gary to discover his hidden talent as a salesman. Thus, a new chapter began in their lives, one in which important life lessons would begin to manifest themselves.

Without a degree and armed only with Gary's gift for sales, the couple began to raise their little family, with only faith as their capital. Gary was the sole breadwinner, selling life insurance, while Ann raised their two small children and ran the household. They lived from paycheck to paycheck, struggling to make ends meet. This financial challenge was a catalyst for Gary and Ann to alter their way of thinking. They were living by faith in a grown-up world where they hardly knew the rules. They did have their Bible as a rule book and a relationship with Jesus, but this did not put dinner on the table. Like many young couples, they could not have made it without the help of their parents. Their friends helped too. But Gary and Ann were uncomfortable being helped by friends. They instinctively knew that if they were going to survive as a family, they would need to be able to prosper on their own, supported by their faith in God.

Gary's Four Lessons

The First Lesson: *Seek first the kingdom of God.*
Matthew 6:33

For a number of years they couldn't seem to get anywhere, no matter how hard they tried. One afternoon while Ann was fixing dinner, Gary looked out the sliding glass doors of their home across the yards of the neighborhood, and said to Ann, "What we are seeking is not so unique or special. Look out there at all the TV antennas and cars in the driveways. They all want the same thing: to own their own home, send their kids to college, retire, buy a retirement home at the lake, and die. What's so unique about that?"

Ann stepped over to the door to look too and said, "Yes, you're right! What does God want us to do? That's what's important. We need to pray to discover what his plan is."

Gary said excitedly, "This is what is missing in our lives, and this is why we can't seem to get out of this rut of just making it month to month. I don't want to achieve the American dream and look back and think, did we ever do anything eternal? Did we take the time to do something significant?" They decided to put God first and ultimately got the call to enter the ministry and go into the mission field. They didn't know where, but thought bible school would be a good start. They found an advertisement for a ministry school in Tulsa and decided to pursue the idea.

The Second Lesson: *Abraham and Sarah and the Ishmael experience.*
Genesis 15 & 16

They began making plans to move the family to Tulsa. Little did they know what would transpire, but looking back they realized they had an attitude much like that of Abraham and Sarah. When God promised them a son, rather than believe God and wait for the promise to come to pass, they took it into their own hands and had a son conceived through their maidservant. They did not believe that Sarah could have a child of her own, being past the child-bearing years. So Abraham took a maidservant to have his promised child. However, this would not be a child of promise, but instead a child of his own making, with disastrous results.

Having sold everything, Gary and Ann devised a plan to go to a bible college in Tulsa by way of Idaho. They wanted to clear up some debts before going to school. Gary's brother and his wife offered to help by inviting them to live with them in Idaho, where Gary had a job waiting. They could live rent-free and work to pay off their debts before going to college. Seemed like a good idea at the time, so without praying about it, they headed from Florida to Idaho. The promised job did not transpire, the families living together did not work very well, and they were trapped in a winter that they had never experienced before.

They believed that God led them to attend bible college, but it turned out to be their Ishmael experience. He explained it this way, "It was like telling God, 'I know what you want us to do; now let me show you how we are going to do it.'" Once they decided to go to Tulsa, they should have prayed and gotten God's direction and plan to get there debt free. This was their second big life lesson in this journey of faith.

After six long months of an Idaho winter with nothing working out, they finally realized what they had done. Once they got back on God's plan, it took no time at all to get local jobs and save enough to buy a large old SUV and pack it with all they had left of their worldly possessions.

They landed in Tulsa and Gary woke up early the next day to a rainy, overcast morning. When he woke Ann up, she burst into tears. "What do we do now?" They realized that they had no jobs, friends, or family in Tulsa. They were alone, and for the first time ever they now had to depend on God for everything! Later that same day, Gary was offered a job and found housing and a church that had a bible college. By the third month, Gary and Ann were attending Victory Bible Institute. After his initial job, Gary found a good job selling furniture just across the street from the college. Ann found a great opportunity to manage a retail fabric store. These were not bad jobs while attending college; they were making more money than they ever had.

The Third Lesson: *Where God guides, God provides.*
Billy Joe Daugherty

After graduation, the job of finding the place where God wanted them to serve as missionaries became a matter of prayer. They thought God was leading them to Belize, so they briefly visited to "spy out the land," as Joshua and Caleb did in the land of Canaan. They discovered that attaining the funding to return there as missionaries was not as easy as they thought.

Rather than learn from experience, they chose to learn from obedience. The founding pastor of Victory Bible Institute, Billy Joe Daugherty, always said, "Where God guides, God provides." They learned in bible college that he who did not provide for the needs of his own family was worse than an infidel. (See 1 Timothy 5:8.) So this time they prayed about it. They decided to obey the Word by providing for their family needs by returning to work while waiting to hear from God. One morning, while browsing the classified columns for jobs, Gary discovered a want ad: *Work for God and earn a commission.* He called the listed phone number. It was a job opportunity to sell advertising at a Christian television station founded by the notable missionary, Dr. Lester Sumrall, who was led, as he was nearing retirement, to develop a worldwide media ministry after ending his work in the mission field.

In 1987 Gary entered what he describes as some of the best years of his life. He was chosen for the sales position with LeSEA Broadcasting, a Christian family station where he started out in sales, eventually becoming General Manager. "I loved the work—it was me," Gary said, smiling. He learned about broadcasting, advertising, and all aspects of the media business.

Although he was a manager operating in a secular position, Gary always considered it "a ministry of helps," as spoken of in the Bible. He loved that his work helped to provide the funding to preach the Gospel in homes across America and the world. It was missionary work, but in the domestic mission field. The company was broadcasting the Gospel into the homes of a wide variety of families, many unlikely to have previously entered a church. In the Post Christian Era, it was a cross-cultural mission, a mission field he would have never imagined he would serve. After 12 years serving the ministry of LeSEA, Gary moved on to start his own advertising and media business with his son as a partner. The business expanded quickly, serving both religious and commercial clients, growing to 14 employees and over $1,000,000 annually in revenue.

The Fourth Lesson: *Count it all joy when life tests you!*
James 1:2-4

In 2007, after a very successful run, the economy became unstable. The business began to stumble due to ad budget cutbacks, and then a key employee left with three large clients. The company was in a serious crisis, but Gary refused to declare bankruptcy. He attempted to borrow to get past the rough financial situation, but that strategy ultimately failed. In 2008 Ann and Gary lost their home to foreclosure. Gary explained, "The advertising business is high risk and fraught with many variables. When a business is down financially, the first thing that is cut is their advertising budget. Additionally, a small-business owner like myself must keep their eye on the ball regarding employee problems and expenses. My company lost a lot of money fast." Regardless of the stresses, God was faithful and they were faithful to God, as they slowly worked their way out of the situation.

Gary and Ann put their faith to the test and did what the Bible says to do in times of crisis: Love your enemies, pray for those who despitefully use you, and move forward with joy when you find yourself in trials and tribulations. They learned the truth of the bible verse that had been part of their wedding ceremony 44 years before: *...a threefold cord is not easily broken...* (Ecclesiastes 4: 9-12) They weathered the storms and with God woven into their lives their marriage grew even stronger as they helped each other through the challenges of life.

Gary's media business has gone through several major economic crises: the dot-com bubble, the banking crisis of 2007 and 2008, and other economic downturns that resulted in loss of clients. In addition, they failed at several attempts at other ventures to bail the business out. They prevailed each time through an optimistic, hopeful outlook and prayer for guidance. They believed it most important to live out their Christian faith and principles in front of their children, grandchildren, and business associates.

There were other challenges. During their time of financial stress, Gary's mother died tragically from a severe stroke, and Ann's mother succumbed to Alzheimer's. Gary set forth their tenet. "We have hope, and we hang on tightly to God. We grieved deeply, but we moved on positively with hope in the Lord." Ann proclaimed, "God has been faithful to us. We are blessed with children and grandchildren, who live close to us. We love them so much and enjoy them immensely." Gary added, "We're very happy and filled with joy always. We have the most important things in life—good friends and family who live nearby. And did you know that our advertising business is ranked in the top three in Tulsa?"

In the four years we have known Gary and Ann, we have never heard negative words of regret, anger, or self-pity, even when serious business or family issues have arisen. Although they are both busy with their careers, they are active in church and helping others. Gary mentors distressed youths in the Tulsa Boys Home, effectively helping the troubled adolescents, using his strengths of evangelism and sales. Along with Ann, he serves as president of the India Gospel Foundation: a non-profit doing mission work in India with an orphanage, a bible school, and evangelistic outreach providing relief and medical services to rural villages. Gary, a dedicated Christian, believes the Lord suddenly altered his life from a self-destructive path to one of purpose, hope,

Gary & Ann today.

and love—a born-again miracle. Gary testified, "I love God above all else, and I love my neighbor as myself. No matter how great the battles and how exciting the victories, I maintain the greatest hope of all—to have our names written in The Lamb's Book of Life."

Quite a transformation for a man who emerged from a self-destructive, troubled youth to become a successful self-made business man with a happy family, achieving the transformation through his passionate, determined adherence to the principles of Christianity.

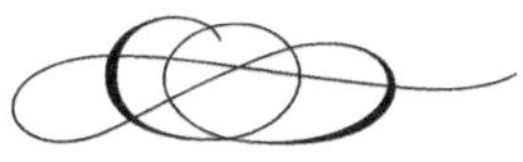

Chapter 11

Turning Losses into Wins

By Sean Kouplen

My name is Sean Kouplen, and this is my story, which I hope will help lead others out of despair to hope.

In 2008, at the age of 34, I had the opportunity to realize my lifelong dream of purchasing a financial institution. As you can imagine, this was both terrifying and exciting. About five years earlier, I had written "to own a bank" as one of my top five life goals, but I really never thought it would happen. Typically, when a financial institution sells, another larger financial institution purchases it. The regulators are very nervous about outside investor groups purchasing banks, and I was only 34 years old at the time. Plus, how would I gather the millions of dollars necessary to purchase and recapitalize the bank?

At 34, I was among the youngest individuals ever to lead the purchase of a bank, and I had huge plans. The first six months were so much fun as I got to know our new employees, finalized our strategic plan, and began to recruit new clients. Unfortunately, by the fall of 2008, my excitement turned to panic when it became obvious that the global economic collapse, The Great Recession, wasn't going to spare Regent Bank.

The Great Recession of 2008-2010 was the most severe economic collapse our country had seen since the Great Depression of the 1930s. Caused primarily by mortgage defaults due to faulty underwriting and the selling of mortgage-backed securities all over the world as Triple A rated paper, this collapse caused credit and consumer demand to dry up. Globally, trillions of dollars in global wealth evaporated, hundreds of banks were closed, and the Dow Jones Industrial Average dropped from 14,000 to 6,000 in a matter of months.

Banks operate on a very thin profit margin, and when you are unprofitable like we were, the margin for error was even thinner. Banks are required to maintain minimum capital ratios and ours were dropping rapidly. We continued to grow our assets, and our earnings were declining due to unexpected loan losses. I believed things were going to turn around, but the evidence pointed to the contrary.

Unfortunately, there were only two ways to augment our capital position: increased earnings or outside investment. Neither of these appeared very likely. Our earnings continued to slide, despite our efforts to cut costs, because we kept losing money on loans. Outside investment seemed unlikely because virtually everyone's net worth was dropping fast with no end in sight, and we were all concerned with our own survival. Investing good money after bad money in Regent Bank just did not seem very logical. Angela and I were tapped. We had already invested everything we had into the bank and I had gone without a paycheck, or a reduced paycheck, for months.

By February of 2009, things looked hopeless, and I was facing the realization that Regent Bank might not survive. Worse than this, I was becoming increasingly depressed. Twenty-hour work days and the inability to eat or sleep were making me despondent. My wife, friends, and pastor were supportive, but I could not escape the truth. I prayed for hours on end that God would take our money but not the money of the innocent people who had invested with me. My thoughts constantly turned to my friends and family, who had each invested a minimum of $100,000, not on Regent Bank, but on Sean Kouplen. It was a nightmare.

I wasn't sure who to turn to, so I called my mentor Gordon Greer. Gordon grew up in my hometown of Beggs, Oklahoma and has been the chairman of the largest bank in Kansas and Oklahoma during his distinguished banking career. Gordon was now semi-retired, in his late 70s or early 80s, and always willing to spend time me, providing advice when I needed it. I asked if he would meet me for breakfast; he agreed to meet me at First Watch near 81st and Lewis in Tulsa at seven the following morning.

When I walked into our favorite breakfast spot, Gordon was already there reading the *Tulsa World*. I will never forget his first comment when I walked up: "Good God, Kouplen. You look like hell!" My retort back to him was absolutely true: "Gordon, the sad part is that I feel twice as bad as I look." I sat down and began to tell him about the last six months and how everything had gone terribly wrong. I told him how depressed I was and how difficult it was to get out of bed in the morning. I was a very different person than the "Boy Wonder" he had called me as I ascended my way up the banking ladder.

"Gordon, I don't know what to do," I lamented. "Have you ever been through anything like this?" Gordon Greer then began to tell me about the 1980s in great detail. This was by far the most challenging banking era in Oklahoma due to a substantial crash in oil prices at the same time the Federal Reserve drastically increased interest rates. This created a death spiral that very few survived. "Sean, for over three years I never had a good day at work. Because of the widespread defaults, people were desperate and angry at the banks. Very seldom did a day go by that I wasn't cursed, slandered, assaulted, or sued by someone. It was simply awful."

"So, how did you survive this terrible period?" I asked. I was desperate for some advice that could keep me going, and I got it.

"Sean, here is what I learned," explained Gordon. "Every morning, I would get up and get ready for work. I would eat my oatmeal and drink my coffee, and I would read the paper. As I was ready to leave my home, I passed an oval-shaped mirror to the right of the door leading to the garage. I would look at myself in that mirror, and I would tell myself, 'Gordon, do the very best you can do today.' This was all I could do." Gordon said he would then drive to work and experience all of the terrible situations mentioned earlier. It often felt like the misery would never end. But at the end of the day he would drive back home, pull into his garage, walk in the door and ask himself one simple question, "Gordon, did you do the best you could do today?" If the answer was yes, that was all he could do. He couldn't control oil prices, interest rates, or how other people treated him. All he could do was his best. "Sean," Gordon said, "You can't control this global economic collapse, your loans going bad, or whether the FDIC is going to shut you down. All you can do is your best."

Wow, this simple advice changed my life forever. I realized that the one thing I could control was myself and my effort, and that was all it took. Immediately, I changed my perspective and began doing my best. I started getting sleep, exercising, and eating right. Through prayer, I fought the feelings of fear and depression that constantly tried to overtake me. I was doing better, but the reality of Regent Bank's impending failure was still there.

On February 17, 2009, I was attending our small community church in Bixby, Oklahoma. I taught the adult Sunday school class, and my wife taught the kids. We both got out a little late, and since the auditorium was full, ended up sitting in the front row. As the choir was singing "Healer" and they came to the words "I believe you're my healer. I believe you're more than enough for me," I became very emotional. For the first time in my life, I was not sure that God was my healer. My problems seemed too great for even him. Suddenly, I heard the very clear words "Do you believe I am your healer?" I looked around, thinking someone was playing a joke on me, but there was no one there. My wife was the closest person to me and she was singing. I believe God spoke to me that day.

Two days later, on February 19, 2009, I was at our bank in Nowata, Oklahoma, and Sandy Moore and I were about to deliver 80 letters to our shareholders. These letters stated that I was extremely sorry about the performance of the bank, but we needed $3 million in additional capital or we were in danger of closing. As Sandy was about to walk out the door with this tray of letters, I became overcome with nausea. This was admitting failure, and all of my fears were coming true. I also seriously doubted whether anyone would invest additional money in such a challenging economic time.

Suddenly, as Sandy was walking toward the door, the phone rang and our receptionist, Arlene, answered it. "Sean, the United States Treasury Department is on the phone for you." My stomach sank. I told Sandy not to send the letters because it might be too late. Sandy began to cry, and I began to cry. As I took the longest recorded 15-foot walk in history, I knew my life was about to end.

I stared down at the blinking light on my phone and finally gathered the courage to pick it up. A serious female voice on the other end said, "Mr. Kouplen, my name is Lisa Taylor. I'm with the U.S. Treasury Department. How are you today?" Did she want the truth? "Ms. Taylor, I guess that all depends on how this phone call goes," I replied. She chuckled, I think. I couldn't really hear because my heart was beating out of my chest. "Mr. Kouplen, I am calling today about our Capital Purchase Program. You may not be interested in this, but the U.S. Treasury has chosen Regent Bank as one of a few select community banks in the country, and we would like to invest up to $3 million in your bank." Yes, $3 million. I tried to control my emotions because I didn't want to scare her away, but I could not stop crying. It was a miracle.

Regent Bank has now grown into one of the country's top community banks. We have grown from 43 employees to almost 100, from one location to four, and from $72 million to $500 million in assets. But I will never forget the tremendous challenges we faced in 2008-2010, the wisdom of Gordon Greer, and the goodness of a God who saved us.

None of this would have been possible, however, if we had given up. I believe that every day there is a spiritual battle for our mind. We can choose to trust in God and focus on abundance, gratitude, peace, joy and love. Or, we can allow Satan to control our mind and focus on scarcity, fear, anxiety and worry. We must train ourselves to start each day by anchoring ourselves to God and approaching the day with a positive mindset.

God led me to start a daily devotional to help us all start our day the right way. Every weekday from 8:17 a.m. to 8:30 a.m., thousands of callers anchor themselves to him by calling 888.630.4807 and listening in.

The truth is, we simply don't have as much control as we think we do. As Mr. Greer taught me, we just need to do our best every single day and leave the results up to God. That's all we can do.

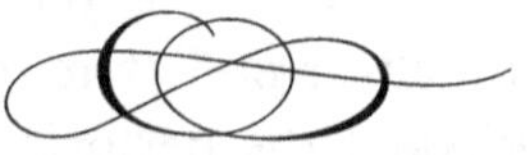

In a chat with Sean about success in business, he observed, "Nearly all successful people in business and sports believe they have a purpose designed by God. We make the best of what God has given us." Note that Sean defines success as providing a service to a client or partner, whereby their needs are met in a business agreement. His goal is to help people, rather than to simply make as much money as possible.

In Sean, I have seen a leader, a person of high emotional intelligence. Like others with a high "EQ," he is clear about his life purpose and values.

- He cultivates self awareness, listening to himself and to others.

- He shows empathy and encourages others, focusing on the positive.

- He's stress-resilient through his faith.

- He keeps good company

Sean has turned a loss into a win. He has gone on to lead and to instill this approach in his employee teams and associates. There are now four Regent Banks, each with a happy team, which makes the company invincible. This is his secret ingredient for himself and his employees.

At a recent business luncheon, Sean gave a presentation to advocate his philosophy of managing a business for success. He applies "The Way of Love," as explained in 1 Corinthians 13:4-6: *Love is patient and kind; love does not envy or boast; it is not arrogant or rude. It does not insist on its own way; it is not irritable or resentful; it does not rejoice at wrongdoing, but rejoices with the truth.* He believes the keys to good leadership and a good company come from the bible. In fact, Sean begins his day leading a daily devotional, to which over 2,000 people call in each morning. Leading with fear results in poor leadership. Leading with love results in great leadership. He uses the following strategies for leading with love:

- Give praise to reinforce positive behavior. There should be three praises for one criticism.

- Be consistent in applying your values and principles.

- Be kind; show that you care for your team members. Focus more on the team than on yourself.

- Being trustworthy earns the confidence and respect of others. Always be truthful and transparent. Hire the best, most trustworthy people.

- Celebrate wins and accomplishments; don't focus on mistakes or wrong-doing.

- Don't micromanage but trust people to do their jobs.

- Listen well; don't insist on your own way or be resentful.

- Don't be arrogant, rude, and irritable.

Sean practices these key wisdoms for achieving happiness and success at home and in life:

- Remain fixed on the good and see your problems as opportunities. Turning losses into wins is the mark of a happy, successful champion.

- With fortitude and determination, anything is possible.

- Positive attitude is what determines your day. Choosing a positive attitude provides you with confidence, vibrant health, and true beauty.

- Helping and encouraging others to emerge from darkness to a hopeful, happy self awareness will give you joy.

Chapter 12

A Miraculous Survival

The truck struck me violently from behind, without warning, as Nancy and I were crossing the street near Utica Square. She shrieked with horror as she watched me being thrown into the air, landing on my head 20 feet away as she was narrowly missed. She screamed, "Stop! Stop! Stop! Don't run over my husband!" She rushed to my side; I was crumpled on the pavement, bleeding, and apparently dead. We had been enjoying a magnificent, sunny fall day, with brilliant red and yellow autumn foliage everywhere. In an instant of negligence by the pickup driver, our lives were literally smashed.

St. John hospital was just two blocks away, and an ambulance arrived quickly. A pulse was detected. I was rushed to ER. Nancy was shaking and crying, trying to pull herself together to call the children, Jamie and Megan. A team of doctors worked quickly to assess the extent of damage. Hemorrhaging was occurring in the brain, causing pressure that could soon result in death. A scan of my skeletal system showed a severe skull fracture and five broken vertebrae.

The lead doctor related my status to Nancy. "He is alive. He has suffered a severe concussion and skull fracture. Bleeding is occurring in and around his brain. We are attempting to treat that. Does he take blood thinners?" the doctor asked

"Yes," Nancy answered. "Is that a problem?"

The doctor was apologetic as he said, "If the bleeding continues inside his skull, he could die soon. And even if he survives, he's probably going to lose all memory. We must stop the bleeding." Nancy was grief-stricken and still suffering from the trauma of the accident. She began to sob again. The doctor asked, "Ma'am, can you tell me what the type and dosage of the blood thinner is?"

Nancy completed the necessary paperwork. She called the children again to let them know that I was alive but in critical condition. She emailed and texted close friends. Support began arriving soon with our daughter, Megan, and our grand-daughter Audrey. I remember nothing of that day from the time I was struck by the pickup. Apparently, I was transitioned from testing in the emergency room to ICU, occasionally throwing up blood.

The next morning I awoke briefly to the sounds of beeping monitors and the wailing of an ambulance siren just outside. Nancy, who had been by my bedside all night, noticed and asked hesitantly, "How do you feel?"

"I have a splitting headache," I said groggily. Where am I? What happened?" I asked slowly.

Nancy smiled and exclaimed, "You know me! You've been run into by a pickup, and you're recovering in an intensive care unit at St John Hospital. You're on strong narcotic pain medication. You have a severe head injury, which caused bleeding in your brain and a buildup of pressure. That's what's giving you the headache. It's Saturday morning, and you can have visitors if you choose. You also have five fractured vertebrae. You won't be able to get out of bed without assistance and pain. Are you hungry for breakfast?"

Pastor Tom from our Methodist Church soon visited. We chatted a bit, but what I said did not make much sense. He laid his hands on my leg and began to pray for me, calling on the Lord to heal me. A positive, life-giving energy began to stir within me.

That Saturday and Sunday, friends and family poured into ICU. They definitely did not come for conversation with me. They came to bring their love and healing prayers. As a group together laid their hands on me and prayed, I could feel the posi-tive, loving energy moving through my body. A miracle was beginning to unfold. My life and memory were going to survive the traumatic accident of being violently run down by a pickup truck. They made life worth living. They were a key part of a miracle.

I was determined then and there to survive and rebuild physically and mentally. With fortitude, determination, and the Lord, anything is possible. The incident occurred on November 17th, 2017. By New Year's I was off the walker, but still using walking sticks. By March, I was released from wearing the back brace with all verte-brae completely healed and no surgery. At that time I was also released from physical therapy and speech therapy. By mid-April the dizziness finally subsided, and I began to lift weights at the gym to rebuild. By July I began hitting a golf ball again, which the doctor had thought was unlikely. Today, eight months later, I feel terrific, can easily walk five miles in hills, can lift my heaviest honey bee hives, and have regained my mental and physical stamina.

I again became active in mentoring at the Tulsa Boys Home, starting with a session based on my accident and recovery. I talked about the necessity of good, strong relationships and a deep faith in order to survive and make life worth living. As previously discussed, these adolescents had all encountered abusive home situations or had no home at all, leaving them scarred as if they had PTSD. My experience was shown to be a part of God's plan for me to help others from darkness to light, making a positive, happy difference. We ended with a discussion of how the horrific accident was actually a blessing, a light, part of God's plan.

Life can end in an instant; we must be good with the Lord and with other people, living life to the fullest. My faith has changed my life in many positive ways, making seemingly impossible goals attainable.

My illnesses and serious accidents have brought me closer to God and made me appreciate life more than ever.

Chapter 13
Making Life Worth Living

Ted Robertson is a respected, beloved pillar of the Tulsa community, well known for his generosity and kindliness, his business, Robertson Tire, and his organization, Tulsa Christian Businessmen (TCB). He has helped countless others, especially those in stress. He is a happy, contented, and loving married man who has been retired since 1999.

Ted was born into a Christian family. When he was 16, his father died, and Ted admits, "I began to hate God." The loss of his father, who was only 38, was the beginning of an extremely dark and troubled time for him. He did not like church people. He did not like himself. At 27 he met and married a beautiful woman who was a devout Christian. They soon had a child.

Ted worked as a salesman for General Tire. He typically entertained vendors by taking them out to nightclubs, sometimes every night of the week, a behavior not conducive to a happy family life. After four years, he reached the low point in his marriage and moved out of his home for 45 days, leaving his wife and two sons.

"I was experiencing hell, a lesson on separation from God," Ted said. He decided to go back to God and to his wife if she would have him. She took Ted back on condition that he go to church. They went to a Pentecostal church, where the preacher and God called him, and a miracle happened. He was immediately struck with the love of God, as well as himself, his wife and children, and many others. "All the past bitterness toward my mother and church people disappeared. Even my bad cigarette habit melted away. Suddenly I loved those church people," said Ted. Anna welcomed Ted back into the now loving home, where he and Anna had two more children, all now living in a very happy relationship.

Ted's life changed positively in many ways. He called those with whom he was going out to nightclubs and told them he would no longer be joining them. He began building deep relationships, which led to success in business, family, and the community.

Ted had started a tire business, but it was doing poorly. At the time, tires were distributed to service stations, where they were mounted on cars. He owed $72,000, which was past due. He considered filing bankruptcy. It was another dark time. But his bank and tire supplier backed him, and he decided to do the right thing, which turned out to also be the smart thing.

He developed a new business plan for a tire store where customers could buy tires and have them mounted on the spot, eliminating the middle-man distributor. Within 18 months his debtors were paid off. Ted said, "I have never taken the easy, non-Christian path of bankruptcy. I did not run from my problems, but faced the problems and let God help me."

"As my relationships with my funders and the community grew stronger," Ted explained, "my business began to grow exponentially." Robertson Tire has now grown from $47,000 a year to $30,000,000 a year. Ted gives God the credit for his success. Stress was removed when his focus changed from making money to helping and giving value to his customers, his suppliers, and his employees. Ted began managing his business and himself with integrity and generosity, according to Christian principles. He loves his family, nurturing the children to follow and become part of Robertson Tire, ultimately managing 17 tire stores today.

Ted's Ten Principles of Life and the Tire Business

1. Don't leave home without a spare. Be prepared for the unexpected. Have a plan B.

2. Keep well balanced. Don't hit the curb. If you do, fix it.

3. Keep cool to avoid blowouts. Overheating puts you and others in danger.

4. Avoid the potholes in life: strife and being unforgiving lead to ruin.

5. Don't drive on your rims. Know when to stop—before you get stopped.

6. You will get what you pay for. Don't be cheap! Give the best. Expect the best.

7. For long life, rotate regularly. Recreation is important. Have fun.

8. Keep a puncture-proof attitude: be positive. Learn how to handle small irritations quickly.

9. Have a weekly attitude alignment. Visit a House of God regularly.

10. Be an all-weather person—enjoy the good times; learn from the bad times.

Ted initiated the Tulsa Christian Businessmen to bring together the Tulsa business community in fellowship. Speakers are brought in to set forth business practices aligned with Christian principles. Police, judges, attorneys, prison wardens, politicians, managers of public facilities, and charities are invited to speak on Christian values as applied in their disciplines. The organization has been a vital part of the Tulsa business community for over 28 years.

Tragedy struck the Robertson family in 1992 when Ted's wife, Anna Kate, whom he loved dearly, died of ovarian cancer. As the family suffered deeply from the loss, Ted asked for help from God and close friends. Ultimately, his loss resulted in contentment. He explained, "With realization of God's will for me, my grief and anxiety diminished." Ted had hope; he chose to be happy and to love others, rather than languish in self-pity. Ted remarried to a friend of his late wife, a friend of the family named Jo Ann. She had also lost her spouse. They met through grief-sharing, fell in love and have enjoyed 26 blessed years together. Jo Ann became Ted's companion and supports his marketplace ministry.

Ted Robertson today.

Ted and his wife, now in their twilight years, live in a retirement village. He looks back at his life as well-spent—building a business in which he established a culture based on Christian principles, a culture in which employees are valued and important, a culture in which employees give customers value, and even though pay is incentive based, do not sell them something they do not need. Employees must give value to the company, and the company will compensate them. Robertson Tire is a happy company, with only minor turnover of managers and low turnover among mechanics. The company is seemingly ironclad, making it more than competitive with today's discount sales businesses. "Christian life does lead to success and joy," says Ted.

Today Robertson Tire supports more than 200 charities and community organizations like the Salvation Army, Boys & Girls Clubs of America, Cherokee Heritage Center, Operation Smile (a worldwide nonprofit performing surgery on children with cleft palates), and Eternal Life Clinic (a medical clinic for poor and underserved people). Yet Ted isn't comfortable resting on his laurels with what he accomplished. He is pouring himself into the next generation, recently starting the Young Businessmen's chapter of the TCB, with business members generally in their twenties and thirties.

Ted is now wholly dedicated to helping others. "This gives me joy, happiness, and more deep relationships," he says. "The last ten percent of my life is a time when I am most effective doing the work that the Lord wants me to do." Ted continuously encourages and helps people who are down and in darkness.

As we sat together in his retirement village discussing his life, Ted regularly waved to friends and associates passing by, inspiring them with words of encouragement and happiness, along with an infectious smile. He takes the same positive, loving attitude to the TCB meetings and to the Pentecostal Church of which he is a member. He tells of many instances of giving help and showing kindness to others that resulted in a positive outcome for everyone. He stated, "I find pleasure in doing little things for people, encouraging them when they are sad. Those little things can be the biggest part of their hearts and often result in rewarding friendships. Everyone has three basic needs: 'Someone to love, something significant and useful to do, and something to hope for.' " His greatest hope, to go to heaven, leaves him contented and happy as he believes his spirit will live on in ultimate joy and bliss forever after he passes away.

Even though Ted had two painful losses in his life—his father and his wife, he no longer becomes depressed over them. Instead he lives on with joy, inspiring happiness and love in many others, often through testimonies to individuals or even large groups. Part of his legacy consists of a successful business based on Christian principles. He remains a pillar of the business and Christian communities, helping many and loved by many.

In the human journey, we all have highs and lows, sometimes extreme lows, just like Ted. But through the physical and emotional challenges of dark times, we must never give up, but maintain hope and move forward with fortitude. Then, in a modified life after a difficult, dark time, and with positive attitude, bounce back to be happy, successful, and of help to others. The life-giving love of God, friends, and family are essential. In Ted's life he has felt anxiety, loss, fear, hurt, disappointments, and betrayals. He has learned from them and by seeking the light in the darkness, he has found hope and contentment, enjoying a happy life worth living.

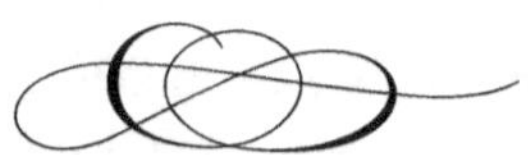

Chapter 14

Jim Stovall's Story

You can envision a bigger and more personally fulfilling destiny for your life. And what you begin to see you can begin to have.
Jim Stovall

Jim Stovall's story demonstrates accomplishing success and having hope and joy even though he became visually impaired at age 28. He related his story to me during several phone discussions and supported his story by providing the names of a couple of the thirty inspirational books he has authored. He set out to become a professional football player, but a major setback changed the trajectory of his life. Now, even though he did not set out to become a writer, he is the author of 30 books. Among these are the bestselling novel, *The Ultimate Gift,* which has been made into a movie starring James Garner and Abigail Breslin, and the inspirational work, *You Don't Have to be Blind to See.* I met Jim after one of his dynamic, inspirational talks, after which he agreed to share his story to follow. This account is the fruit of several phone discussions with Jim.

Jim was born into a Christian family and had what he describes as a normal childhood, even though he lost both a brother and sister (leukemia) at a young age. Then, at seventeen, in the course of a routine physical, Jim was diagnosed with a degenerative eye disease that would lead to total blindness. He was informed that it was not curable. Jim said, "Jeff, I was absolutely devastated, quickly becoming quite depressed. But one night I wandered into an open, dark, empty hall and sat down to think, to assess my life options going forward. The hall eventually began to fill, and I found myself at a Ray Charles concert.

"This was a key transformation for me. Ray gave a great performance, inspiring me with his music. He was blind, of course, but you wouldn't know it from watching his enthusiastic, emotionally-charged singing performance. The audience did not care that he was blind; they cared only about his performance, that he could play music they loved. I learned that a blind person, or anyone with some kind of disability, must take blindness out of what they want to accomplish. In other words, you must separate how you will achieve your goal from what you want to accomplish. I have a choice and decided not to allow blindness to limit me. In fact, I manage to 'read' an audio book a day and have done so for thirty years."

In a meeting with Ray in Madison Square Garden, Ray mentioned that he did not want the word "blind" in his obituary. Neither does Jim. Jim would rather be remembered as a genuine, kind, and loving man.

When Jim graduated from Oral Roberts University, he realized there was no place in corporate America for a blind person, so he considered developing his own business and working for himself. He has succeeded in achieving that dream.

At twenty-nine, Jim became totally blind, triggering a spiritual and emotional crisis. He had been told that it takes a minimum of thirteen months to get through such a crisis before making any serious decisions. In the beginning, he felt sorry for himself and became seriously depressed. He moved into a room in the back of the house and considered just staying there for the rest of his life. He had audio visual equipment for entertainment.

Jim listened to Denis Waitley motivational tapes until he wore them out, but he began to be bored. Fortunately, his career as an athlete gave him the basis, the initiative, and the determination to get things done. One day he decided to play a DVD of a Humphrey Bogart movie that he had watched several times before he became blind. But he could not recall several scenes and became frustrated with his inability to actually see the whole movie. He voiced his frustration to himself. *Somebody ought to do something about this.* As a budding entrepreneur he thought, *How can I help others avoid the problem? I will be that somebody. I will help the blind to 'see' movies, to 'read' books.* "I began right then to develop the concept of making TV available to blind people," Jim said. He knew that people would give you a lot if you could help them solve their problems. Jim had lost his eyesight, but he never lost that vision of helping others to attain a successful life.

Jim founded Narrative Television Network, which reaches millions of homes through the cable system. Ted Turner helped after Jim asked "the Best" for assistance, and they remain close friends today. He was awarded an Emmy for his innovative work in helping visually impaired people to see television in a new way. Jim offered a little wisdom: "It is very important with whom you surround yourself." For example, another good friend is Steve Forbes, who advised Jim on his book *The Ultimate Financial Plan: Balancing Your Money and Life.*

Today Jim Stovall is highly sought after as an author, a public speaker, and a movie producer. He has an impressive list of accomplishments. He has been a national champion Olympic weightlifter, president of the Emmy Award-winning Narrative Television Network, and the bestselling author of thirty books. *The Ultimate Gift, The Ultimate Life,* and *The Lamp* have all been made into motion pictures. For his work in making television accessible to our nation's thirteen million blind and visually impaired people, the President's Committee on Equal Employment Opportunity selected Jim Stovall as the Entrepreneur of the Year. He was also chosen as the International Humanitarian of the Year, joining Jimmy Carter, Nancy Reagan, and Mother Teresa as recipients of this honor.

Jim Stovall is one of the premier motivational speakers of our time, speaking on the world stage. He is prepared; he rehearses what he intends to say and how he intends to say it. Most importantly, he has something useful and genuine to say. He speaks honestly about what he knows to be true in his life, the principles of which are true in the lives of each of us. He lives his daily life as a man of integrity and quality. He issues the truths and wisdoms he has learned from losing his sight, and in its place gaining a vision of his life as a successful businessman and a man with countless strong, loving relationships. He genuinely seeks to encourage his audiences to discover and pursue a personal destiny of greatness. Steve Forbes, president and CEO of *Forbes* magazine, says, "Jim Stovall is one of the most extraordinary men of our era."

I queried, "Jim, how do you accomplish so much when you are blind?"

Jim philosophized, "Blindness for me is no different than for others who have suffered tragedies like divorce or serious illness. I don't even feel like I am blind. It is useless and counterproductive to allow yourself to feel like a victim. Actually, in losing my sight, I captured vision. We walk by faith and not by sight. The fact is, you are blind too. Everybody is blind in some way. Even if you have the capacity for looking, you may not have the capacity for seeing. One involves a physical ability and the other requires inner vision and creativity. What matters most is your ability to make sense of your life and then to make the most of your life.

Jim briefly discussed important steps he takes each day, "I start each day by making a golden list of ten things for which I am thankful. Nothing bad can continue to exist in the midst of gratitude. Then I plan my day. I 'read' a book a day in addition to managing my businesses. I did not feel I was gifted, so I felt I had to work hard, with passion, to achieve my goals. A person must become internally motivated. One of the hardest things about being blind is no one expects anything from you, so it is self-motivation that is essential for me. I care most about what I think of myself rather than what others think. And I expect much of myself."

For Jim, faith plays a large part, but he explained, "Faith is only part of the equation for joy, happiness, hope, success." Jim believes that he has hope from the Lord. He knew with his Christian upbringing that praying was something beneficial. He said, "I know that God has a plan, and that I should listen to him to have a successful and happy life. I begin each day with a prayer of thanksgiving."

Today Jim works with organizations world-wide, teaching and motivating employees with the following wisdom gained from personal experience.

- Anyone can change their life by changing their mind.

- Anyone can turn dreams into reality.

- Be the best that you can be.

- Take action starting today.

- Find and fulfill your destiny regardless of your circumstances.

Jim explained that a form of blindness that most people have is their inability to make sense of their life and then to make the most of their life. He asked a rhetorical question, "Do you have a vision for your life? Most people don't. If at this time, you don't have an inner ability to see yourself fully or to see yourself as you want to be, you can change, because you do not need to remain that way. You can make a new decision, exercise a new option, choose a new path, and have a new beginning. You can acquire a vision for your personal destiny without waiting for a tragedy to give you a wake-up call. You can create a vision for yourself. Personally, I would rather be the person I am today and be blind than be the person I once was and have my eyesight. Being blind isn't the worst thing that can happen to people. Living without hope is the worst thing."

Jim continues to write books. His early book, *You Don't Have to be Blind to See*, still sells well as it is filled cover to cover with inspirational wisdom. Several of his works of fiction have been made into movies, and the DVD's of these films contain narration for the visually impaired.

Jim spoke of the important factors for success garnered from personal experience. "A person must know what they want to do, what you have a passion for. God will let you know, just listen." Jim has a mission statement. He says, "A written mission is essential for everyone." He also has his own personal definition of success for Jim Stovall, not something written for someone else or by someone else. He is mission-oriented and therefore focuses on what he wants to get done, rather than on how to get it done. He says emphatically, "If the why is big enough, the *how* takes care of itself. When I became blind, I could not drive. I could have worried about this 'how to' and never pursued the Narrative TV career. However, I focused on the 'why'—the passionate dream to develop Narrative TV, for which I knew there would be a large audience and therefore demand. The 'how to' then took care of itself, and I have now traveled over two million miles for speaking engagements and developing the Narrative TV."

Here is Jim's list of the five things for ultimate productivity, leading to personal joy:

1. Define success for yourself—establish your own goals. Then follow your passion to succeed. Achieving your goals according to your defined success will bring satisfaction and happiness.

2. Understand what motivates you.

3. Find the best way to communicate your vision.

4. Implement a style that works best for you. It matters most what you do. And you must connect with everyone.

5. Check on your progress—you need short-term goals that start today.

Jim is a fan of Jim Rohn who said, "Your life becomes the sum total of who you hang around with." Jim is part of an accountability group, a small group of close friends who meet every other week to motivate each other to become better people. They ask themselves questions such as, "Have you abused your power?" They pledge not to lie to each other or themselves. Jim said emphatically, "This small, intimate group of close friends who share mutual respect is a powerful motivator and tool for me and for each of us."

"Jim, are you joyful? Do you have hope?" I asked with a smile. "Oh yes, I'm very happy and hopeful. I do everything that I want to do. I would not trade places with anyone. I have a terrific marriage. I love my career helping people to better their lives. I am thankful for so many things, and I feel blessed every day."

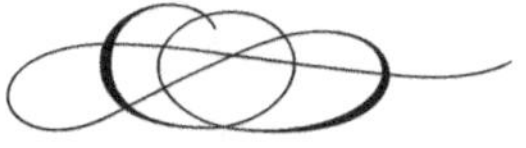

Chapter 15

Open Your Eyes to Joy

"The greatest discovery of my generation is that human beings can alter their lives by altering their attitudes of mind."
William James

Visualizing where you are going is the first step in getting there. If you want to achieve joy, happiness, and success and cultivate hope, fortitude, and a positive attitude, you need to know what they look like. Here are my definitions, based on a Christian perspective.

Joy is a permanent inner contentment with life that is independent of external affairs. It is a state of well-being that supersedes negative emotions. Joy is a condition, a feeling of peace, happiness, pleasure, elation, of contentment with life. It has a positive feel no matter what the circumstances are. It is a positive hope that reaches beyond the current external situation. Christians believe that joy is a gift of God, that accepting Jesus Christ is the key to joy and happiness.

Happiness is a fundamental, natural pursuit in which a person devotes themselves to the things in life that bring them pleasure. Happiness is an emotion with highs and lows. It can never be satisfied. It can be an emotional response to something—like a good joke or winning a footrace. Being happy is a decision that you can make every day. But happiness may vanish in the face of a negative event or a crisis. That's because happiness is temporary. Some words connected with happiness are glee, delight, cheerfulness, gladness, enjoyment, and gratification.

Success has two very different meanings. The first is achieving a favorable or desired outcome. This might be a service you do for others, like empowering them to be successful themselves. For a Christian, success is loving and being loved by others in deep relationships. It is about achieving contentment, hope and joy in your life. Success is defined according to what each person seeks to achieve, which may be a better life following a crisis. This kind of success is not about how much money or personal items are accumulated, as the appetite for these can never be satisfied

The second common meaning of success in the English language is the attainment of popularity or profit. Merriam-Webster defines this as "the attainment of wealth, favor, or eminence." This almost always involves vanity, boastfulness, and concern about one's image. It is not God-centered and therefore fleeting.

Ted Robertson nailed it with his Christian-centered example of success: "When I die and I'm in a casket in the front of the church, if my children and grandchildren walk by and say, 'I want to be just like Dad/Grandpa. I will strive to treat my kids and wife just like he treated us,' then I am a success. And finally, if they think, 'I want to live a life just like Mother and Dad,' then surely I will have led a successful life."

Hope is the virtue of a heart that doesn't lock itself into darkness, that doesn't dwell on the past, that doesn't simply "get by" in the present, but looks to a better tomorrow. Hope is essential to anyone who wants to experience joy and essential for dreaming of a better future. To have hope is not *I hope my team wins* or *I hope I get a raise*. Hope is a "know so," not a "hope so," or wishful thinking. Hope is the knowledge of facts. For example, a Christian believer has hope in the future, because they have trust, extended to the future, in a redeemer, Jesus Christ. Hope is realizing that bad things may happen, but *knowing* that God will be by your side giving you strength.

Positive Thinking will lead you out of the darkest of times. It is the guide to leading a positive life. It means being an optimist, always looking for the good in things rather than being a pessimist, concentrating on the bad things. Negative thinking and speaking keeps one from being happy, while positive thinking has a direct connection with happiness and success.

Fortitude is the strength of mind that enables a person to encounter danger or bear pain or adversity with courage.

How to Open Your Eyes

Promote positive thinking, hopefulness, peace, and happiness within yourself and those around you. But exactly how do I do that, you ask? How *do* I open my eyes? All I can see are closed doors and blind alleys.

You can start by taking baby steps in a positive direction. Positive power is unleashed when you make someone else smile. Today, not tomorrow, step outside yourself and your problems and make someone else feel important. It is better to give than to receive, and it will make you feel better. For example, my editor says she once saw a teenager about to get into his car at the convenience store, when he noticed an old man limping toward the door. The teenager ran all the way across the parking lot to open the door for someone he didn't know and would probably never see again. Both people benefited from the interaction. I wonder if the boy fell asleep that night remembering the surprised smile on the old man's face. Ironically, those of us with our own serious difficulties are the most likely to notice the needs of others and help and nurture them.

You can help others by treating them with dignity and respect. Then they will accept your sincere help. Just being a good listener can make someone's day.

Think positive thoughts and you will get positive results. Even when I was very sick, I thought positively, dreaming of hiking in mountains and enjoying God's wonderful creation. I established impossible goals of hiking again in the mountains with my lovely wife, Nancy. Even though the experts told me I'd be unable to do so, the goal helped me emotionally through many issues. Ultimately, I achieved the goal with absolute joy.

Every time you think positively, you set in motion positive forces resulting in positive outcomes. By thinking differently, you can change your circumstances. Don't passively accept unsatisfactory circumstances. Develop details of the desired outcome, believe in it, work at it, pray about it, visualize it, and actualize it. If you think in negative terms, if you sprinkle your language with negative phrases, you will get negative results. Think in positive terms, and you will achieve positive results. Believe, and you will succeed.

The basic reason a person fails to live a creative and successful life is because of toxic thinking. Successful living comes from reducing the amount of wrong thinking within and increasing the amount of truth, of new, right, healthy thoughts. Truth always produces right actions and therefore, right results. *Ye shall know the truth and the truth will set you free.* (John 8:32)

To remake yourself, cast out those old, dead, unhealthy thoughts, and replace them with new, dynamic, vital, hopeful, and happy thoughts. Listen to yourself and others speak; catch those negative phrases and words; throw them in the trash bin—maybe even write them down first, then tear them up or burn them. Focus on what's good in life and enjoy this moment.

Taking care of yourself is essential, especially if you are a caretaker for someone else. Don't neglect your own needs for those of others. Get adequate sleep. Ben Franklin was right when he said, "Early to bed, early to rise, makes a man healthy, wealthy, and wise." Help yourself to have restful sleep by relaxing, clearing your mind of negative emotions—worries, anger, ill-feelings. Prayer is one way to purge negativity.

Relax in your work and in your play. Watching someone trying too hard at a sport, you will see how stiff, how rigid they appear. Instead visualize yourself relaxing in whatever you do. Take a deep breath and let it out slowly. Setting a routine isn't always possible, but you can strive for it. For example, exercise regularly, preferably daily. A one-hour rigorous walk each day will contribute significantly to physical and emotional well-being. If you don't have time for an hour, walk for ten minutes. You'll be surprised at the results.

Try relaxing with music: classical, romantic, upbeat, or "easy listening." Avoid violent, angry, and harsh, discordant music. Watch movies with happy endings and positive messages. Avoid the horror, violent, and vulgar films. Consider watching Christian movies in which good triumphs over evil, and real inspirational miracles are shown. Turn off the negative political news, especially broadcasts that specialize in slander and hate in order to destroy other people with differing political views, instead of bringing you unbiased facts. Such programs will only make you angry and worried over nothing. Rather, relax with a good book, pleasant classical music, or positive conversation with a good friend.

You can stimulate your creativity and inner feelings of joy by awakening, sharpening, and nourishing your senses. You can think like Leonardo Da Vinci,[1] who each day awakened his five senses. Smell the aroma of a rose; see and enjoy its beauty. Hear lovely, relaxing music. Touch softly, hug another, or take a warm bath. Taste food with exquisite spices. As you smell that beautiful rose or give that special person a hug, you should find yourself smiling and your day becoming a wonderful day.

Start every day by writing down at least five positive things, blessings in your life. If your day starts with children needing immediate attention, write your blessings before you go to bed. Write down three or four good things that

---

1. Michael J. Gelb, *How to Think like Leonardo da Vinci* (Delacorte Press August 1998)

happened that day. Your blessings might be general. For example, you are alive, you have a wonderful partner, you have loving children and grandchildren, good friends. Smile and decide this will be a good day and you will be happy. Instead of saying to yourself, *Today I have to…*, say *Today I get to…* Fill your mind with fresh, new creative thoughts of faith, love, and goodness to remake your life. Flush away your old, worn-out negative thoughts.

Gather inspiring quotes from the Bible and other sources. Stick them on the bathroom mirror, on the refrigerator, or in your wallet, and repeat them often during the day until they become part of you.

With an optimistic attitude and confidence, attack each setback, problem, or obstacle with fortitude and determination. Never, ever give up. Believe it will work out right.

Laugh, be joyful, smile, and encourage others. This approach will help you to win friends, and everyone will have a better day—at work, at home, or at social events. Is your child giving you a hard time? Try looking at them, even if for a few seconds, with unconditional love and acceptance, perhaps remembering the first time you held them in your arms.

Minimize negativism: anxiety, fear, hate, victimhood. When bad things occur and you are consumed with worry or anger, alter your focus entirely. Focus on a pet—your dog or your cat. Or focus on helping others. Let's say you're at the supermarket. Call the clerk by their name. In fact, learn the names of those who serve you. Acknowledge them as individuals. Get outside of yourself, relax, and you can gain a clearer perspective on the worrisome matter.

Be most careful not to let bitter, unhappy people drag you down to their level. Instead, use their behavior as an example of how not to behave and be grateful you are nothing like them. Personally, I avoid these types of people as much as possible. Also, I often choose to not watch the news any more than is necessary to be informed. For example, in politics, especially in high-stakes politics on the national level, today's politicians often attempt to focus your attention on the negative aspects of their opposition. Meanwhile, those in power may be working toward what is best for their constituents or the country. If you step back, think positively, look at the facts, and focus on the good that can result, rather than on the contrived negative, you will lessen your anxiety and anger, even be at peace over the situation.   Often the opposition will express hatred toward those in power. Do not allow yourself to be dragged into this serious negative emotion (and often the consequential behavior), but rather choose to be happy that you and your country are being managed for the better.

Let the past go. Forgive others who have wronged you and forgive your-self. A refusal to forgive opens us to bitterness, opens us to the power of Satan, and blocks us from changing ourselves. Accept what life gives you. Instead of allowing yourself to ruminate over past stumbles, make today a good day and tomorrow a better day.

In summary, you can think your way to failure and unhappiness, but you can also think your way to success and happiness. "A man is what he thinks about all day long," wrote Ralph Waldo Emerson

Reducing Stress

Reducing stress is essential for your physical and emotional well-being. Work without worry, resentment, and tension, but work hard. Irritation, anger, hate, and resentment can have such powerful effects on you that they can produce ill health. The cure is to fill the mind with attitudes of good will, forgiveness, faith, love, and the Holy Spirit.

Negative emotions can cause serious physical and emotional problems. You can make yourself ill, with real physiological symptoms, by giving in to resent-ment, guilt, fear, and anxiety. Victims of chronic physical pain may be suffering from a smoldering grudge, unaware that they bear a chronic resentment. While anger, resentment and guilt make you sick, many physicians tell us that the most up-to-date book on personal well-being is the Holy Bible. When the Bible, the greatest book of wisdom, tells you not to hate or get angry, it is not theoretical advice. In it we can discover what is wrong with us and how to correct our thinking as well.

Anger can be reduced; it can be cooled. Deliberately relax your body, reduce your voice to a whisper, slump down, and relax. Say to yourself, *Don't be foolish, this won't achieve anything, so forget it.* Conjure up a picture of a person of peace. Take three deep breaths and count to ten, or better yet, say the first sentence of the Lord's Prayer. Make a list of everything that irritates you. Then take away each, by prayer if you choose. Your anger will weaken, and you will gain control of it. When angry, train yourself to say, *Is this worth it? It is never worth it to get mad about anything.*

When your feelings are hurt, straighten the situation out as quickly as possible. Don't brood over it and distort it out of proportion. Use spiritual treatment; say a prayer of love and forgiveness. Open your mind and let the grievance flow out. Even go to someone you trust and pour it out to them. Then forget it. Pray often for the person who hurt your feelings until you are free of resentment. Pray that your temper will come under control, that there will be healing peace in your nervous system, as well as in your soul.

Abandon victimhood and self-pity. This trap of agonizing over past negative events and hurts will have serious adverse consequences. Take six steps: forgive, speak the truth, acknowledge your emotions, move from demonizing and let God help you see the other person as a child of God, recognize your complicity in the situation, commit to change and move outside of yourself by helping others. Then, establish a path forward to a positive, good life filled with hope and happiness.

Today's negative news media seeks to convince you that you are a victim, a victim who should be angry, rebellious, and hateful, seeking revenge. Do not fall for this. It will make you anxious, even angry and traumatized. Angry people do angry things to others. You can ruin your life and the lives of others. Instead, alter your outlook to the positive, the good, by helping and loving others.

Reset Your Mind

Believe in yourself. Believe that you can achieve your dreams. After a serious, life-changing crisis, step back and re-evaluate yourself and your goals, your mission in life. You may ask yourself, *What on earth am I here for? What is my destiny?* As Jim Stovall said, "We all are blind in some way."

Create a vision for yourself. We all have creative ideas; cultivate them. Establish a purpose and goals. Everyone can imagine, think, create and dream. It just takes practice. Some morning, right after you wake up and before your conscious mind censors your ideas, make a list of ideas and dreams. Write as fast as you can. It is for your eyes only. The more often you do this stream-of-consciousness writing, the more ideas will come. You may surprise yourself. You must own your own dream and take ownership in your life.

Live your life with hope. Living without hope is the worst thing that can happen to a person. Believe there is a chance for a better tomorrow, starting now. There is a decision you can make, an option you can exercise, a choice you can act on that will make the difference. With hope, what may appear like the end, can be the beginning of a new and better life.

If you don't like the life you are living, change it. Difficult and tough things happen to all of us, but do not allow the past be a stumbling block that dictates your future. When you take responsibility for your life, significant improvement can follow. Don't blame somebody else for where you are in life, but rather, look in the mirror; only you have control of yourself and can make necessary changes. You can make the right decisions, so do not let others do the choosing. No matter how impaired you are as a result of unfortunate circumstances (accident, illness, or other serious loss), you can choose how you will respond and what you will do afterwards. You must understand yourself (accept the new normal of who you are today), like yourself, take charge of your life and then you can pursue your destiny.

Each of the contributors to this book, including myself, has suffered one or more tragedies or crises, including broken relationships, life-threatening illnesses, debilitating injuries, visual impairment, loss of loved ones, life-altering financial losses, depression, or aimless, self-destructive paths as teenagers. Each of them has recovered to achieve a better life, one filled with hope and joy.

The seemingly random things in life—the highs and lows, the successes and failures, the life-threatening illnesses I experienced and beat—are not really so random. All of these were God-scheduled opportunities for growth, self-expression, learning, and for living according to God's plan.

It is a rare person who finds true joy without faith in something bigger than themselves. Committing your life to the Lord, and seeking support in a community of believers can be a significant step in spiritual and physical healing.

Have faith that God, the greatest coach, will lift you to new heights that you could never reach on your own.

> *Faith isn't required as long as you set your goal only as high as the most intelligent, most informed, and expert human effort can reach. Nothing is a miracle until it reaches the area where the utmost that human effort can do still isn't enough. God has to fill that space —that room—between what's possible and what God wants done that's impossible. You don't exercise faith until you have promised more than it's possible to give.*
> Franklin Graham, Rebel with a Cause.

The world offers temporary, short-term answers. Its happiness is fleeting. The whole key to the Christian life is to have what the author and philosopher Dallas Willard called "a well-kept heart." He wrote: "Those with a well-kept heart are persons who are prepared for and capable of responding to the situations of life in ways that are good and right." Jesus said, "Blessed are those who hunger and thirst for righteousness, for they shall be satisfied." (Matthew 5:6) Doing life God's way comes with huge advantages. We need to hunger for the right things, and though we engage the mind, we lead with a heart that is open to the things of God.

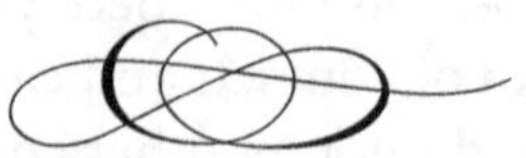

Nuggets of Wisdom
From the Contributors

But the fruit of the Spirit is love, joy, peace, patience, kindness,
goodness, faithfulness, gentleness and self-control.
Galatians 5:22-23

- When you are knocked down, just get up. Don't dwell on your misery, your failures, your anger, or your victimhood.

- We walk by faith, not by sight. Actually, in losing my sight, I captured vision. (Jim Stovall)

- Make sense of your life and then make the most of your life.

- Change your life by changing your mind. Have a fresh start now, or any moment you choose, for what is called failure is not the falling down, but the staying down.

- Make a daily golden list of ten things for which you are thankful. Nothing bad can continue to exist in the midst of gratitude.

- Positive attitude is what determines your day. See problems as opportunities. Choosing a positive attitude provides you with confidence, vibrant health, and true beauty. Smile, it will fill you with energy and peace, and you will become a light to others. See the good and bring out the best in people.

- Envision a bigger, more fulfilling destiny for your life. What you begin to see you can begin to have.

- Your problems are God's opportunities.

- Enjoy the good times, learn from the bad times.

- Turning losses into wins is the mark of a champion.

- With fortitude, determination, and God's help anything is possible.

- Encourage others to emerge from darkness to self-awareness and joy.

- Helping others will bring you joy. It is better to give than to receive.

- Always be truthful and transparent to earn the confidence and respect of others..

- God has a plan for you. Do your best every single day, and leave the results up to God.

- God's love, protection and provision are limitless. Praise him in good times and bad. He will heal you when you come to him with your heart in pieces.

- Relax with positive stimulation of all your senses; good music, tasteful food, beautiful things, pleasant aromas, a hug.

- Enjoy quiet times, walking in the woods and seeing God's wonderful creation, reflecting on his blessings, and your good fortune and blessings.

- Do not harbor ill will toward others who have wronged you. Forgive them and forgive yourself for mistakes you have made.

- Start each day with a prayer to be happy. Choose to be happy.

- Peace ends depression. Peace comes by standing with the Lord, which helps us to endure. Suffering produces endurance, endurance produces character, and character produces hope.

- Practice positive self-affirmation every day to feel happy, improve your self-esteem, and help you feel comfortable in your own skin.

- Your life becomes the sum total of who you hang around with. Choose deep relationships with positive, loving, joyful people.

- You can achieve joy by taking charge of your life and committing to your goals. When you believe that everything that happens in your life is an opportunity provided by God, you will be infused with confidence and a greater sense of purpose.

- God intervened to save me so that I could fulfill his purposes, his greater destiny for me. Possibly this is true for you as well.

- Life's journey consists of darkness (failures, extreme losses) and light (opportunities, successes, loving relationships). The outcomes depend upon your response. When you are knocked down, get up and fight. Things that go wrong can shape you, or they can scar you. You can choose to be positively shaped.

- Avoid chasing material desires. Rather, focus on what is most important in life – love of friends and family.

- Let go of the past. Prisons hold many who sought revenge and ruined their own lives. Remember, life is a gift.

- Serious setbacks like severe illnesses can bring you closer to God and help you to appreciate life more than ever. Learn from them, have empathy for others afflicted and seek to fulfill God's plan for you.

- To achieve joy, fulfill three basic needs: someone to love, something significant and useful to do, and something to hope for.

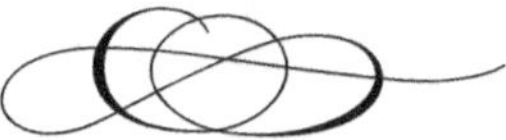

References

Bob Goff, *Love Does* (Nelson Books, 2012)

Scott Hamilton, *The Great Eight; How to Be Happy* (Thomas Nelson; 2nd edition October 11, 2009)

Norman Vincent Peale, *The Power of Positive Thinking* (Simon & Schuster)

Jim Stovall, *You Don't Have to Be Blind To See; Find and Fulfill Your Destiny Regardless of Your Circumstances.* (Thomas Nelson 1996)

Rick Warren, *The Purpose Driven Life; What on Earth Am I Here For?* (Zondervan 2002)